The Ultimate
AIR FORCE
Basic Training Guidebook

Tips, Tricks, and Tactics for
Surviving Boot Camp

Senior Airman
Nicholas Van Wormer

Savas Beatie
California and New York

Cataloging-in-Publication Data is available from the Library of Congress.

First edition, second printing
10 9 8 7 6 5 4 3 2

ISBN-13: 978-1-932714-92-0

SB

Published by
Savas Beatie LLC
521 Fifth Avenue, Suite 1700
New York, NY 10175
Phone: 916-941-6896

Editorial Offices:

Savas Beatie LLC
P.O. Box 4527
El Dorado Hills, CA 95762
Phone: 916-941-6896
(E-mail) sales@savasbeatie.com

Savas Beatie titles are available at special discounts for bulk purchases in the United States by corporations and other organizations. For more details, contact Special Sales, P.O. Box 4527, El Dorado Hills, CA 95762. You may e-mail us about your needs at sales@savasbeatie.com, or you may visit our website at www.savasbeatie.com for additional information.

Front Cover: Tyler Silber

Proudly printed and bound in the United States of America.

This book is dedicated to past, current, and future Airmen.
Thank you for your day-to-day sacrifices to protect our great nation.

Please Note:

The fitness program presented in this book was not designed by a licensed physician. You should consult with a physician before beginning any fitness program or exercises discussed in this book. All forms of exercise pose some inherent risk, even for people in top physical condition. The author, and everyone who contributed to this book, advises readers to take full responsibility for their safety and know their limitations. The statements (and illustrations) in this book are the opinion of the author.

Contents

Contents (continued)

Foreword

I knew absolutely nothing about the military when I entered basic training. I had no military family history and no prior desire to ever join the military. It was on the tragic morning of September 11, 2001, that I realized what I was taking for granted all these years. Freedom, as wonderful as it is, is an uphill struggle and comes with an enormous responsibility. It wasn't so much a decision but a calling, that convinced me to join the military—the Army Reserves.

I left for basic training without an ounce of military knowledge one month after September 11, 2001. However, I used this lack of knowledge to my advantage. I took notes on everything, with the ambition that no recruit would have to go through basic training like I did, with no knowledge of what was in store for me. I listened to hundreds of soldiers share their advice, tips, and tricks on surviving basic training. When I was deployed shortly after basic training to serve in Operation Enduring/Iraqi Freedom, I used what little spare time I had to organize the notes, add to them, and assemble the most practical basic training guide ever written.

The result was *The Ultimate Basic Training Guidebook: Tips, Tricks, and Tactics for Surviving Boot Camp* (Savas Beatie 2005, 2010). My book was designed around my knowledge in the Army, although it is applicable to all branches. The heavy correspondence I have received from people who have used or seen it convinced me that other similar books on the specific branches would be very helpful to many people. The result is Nick Van Wormer's *The Ultimate Air Force Basic Training Guidebook*.

Like my book, Nick's is designed to be straightforward and easy to understand. Read it carefully, write in the book, underline, highlight—whatever it takes to help you learn. I strongly suggest that you take advantage of the fitness routine in this book. Many hours of research and trial and error went toward creating the program. In my opinion there is no other fitness program that can get you in shape for basic training faster. Remember: there is a difference between "civilian fit" and "military fit."

And yes, you should read this book more than once before you leave. If you are heading for the Air Force, you will find Nick's book the most helpful you can read to prepare for your experience.

*   *   *

During World War I, President Woodrow Wilson's staff developed an eight-week course for military recruits. This course, known as basic combat training, taught new soldiers basic survival skills for combat situations. After many decades of trial and error, modern basic training is designed today to physically challenge incoming recruits, test their mental toughness, and get them ready for military service in the finest army the world has ever known.

After your basic training has ended, you will feel and act more confident about yourself than ever before. Basic training will test your capabilities and limits. Your leadership skills will develop. You will be more marketable to future employers. Why? Because smart employers love to have people with a military background apply for job openings. They know what you have successfully accomplished. The environment you will endure at basic training is much more rigorous than any forty-hour work week.

If I Had Only Known . . .

As I was passing through basic training, I realized there was so much I could have prepared for—*if I had only known*. When I completed basic training and began Army Reserve obligations, I discussed this topic with many other soldiers. Each agreed that preparing for basic training in advance of arrival was not only possible, but relatively easy to do—*provided a new recruit knew what to prepare for, and how to prepare for it.*

It is my hope that *The Ultimate Air Force Basic Training Guidebook* fills this need by teaching you what to expect, and how to avoid the most common problems experienced by new recruits. In a major way, this book follows the Six P's maxim: prior planning prevents piss poor performance. Avoiding problems keeps you out of trouble, and staying out of trouble will allow you to develop, thrive, and succeed during basic training.

This book will also provide you with an invaluable training advantage and make your experience in basic training more rewarding. However, it is not designed to teach you *everything* you need to know about basic training. There are two good reasons for this. First, if this book touched on everything from how to march in formation to how to man a defensive fighting position, you would be holding an 800-page instruction manual. Trying to read and memorize all those details would be both discouraging and counterproductive. Instead, *The Ultimate Air Force Basic Training Guidebook* allows you to focus on what is <u>really</u> important; the smaller details will be easy to learn once the main concepts are understood and memorized. Second, it is impractical to learn how to assemble an M-16 rifle or put on chemical gear by reading an instruction manual. These things are best taught with hands-on training in the field.

"Why are you joining the military?" I am sure you have heard that question already; if not, you soon will. It is an important question to consider. Do you know the answer?

The military offers some fantastic incentives for joining, including a paid college education and even retirement pay (with twenty or more years of service). Many people join the military because of these incentives. Perhaps you are down on your luck and need a steady job, so your signed up for active duty; maybe you need some weekend work and signed up for the reserves. As good as these reasons seem, they will not be good enough.

Virtually anyone with prior or current military service will tell you that soldiers who joined because of the steady paycheck often end up unmotivated and frustrated. The greatest satisfaction you will receive from the military is knowing that you are part of an elite fighting force.

You will gain pride, confidence, and the admiration of most of your fellow American citizens. Hopefully, you joined (or are thinking of joining) because you want to serve your country in the greatest military on earth.

Many people enter the service with an inaccurate concept of what it means to be a soldier. Hollywood has embellished the soldier's image by creating movies with gruesome battle scenes. These types of movies sell tickets. No one is going to watch a movie about three soldiers experiencing kitchen duty.

The truth is that during your basic training you will learn how to kill enemy soldiers. That is every soldier's primary objective. However, think about what it takes to send one soldier, or airmen, or Marine, etc. out to kill an enemy target. He needs food, supplies, a vehicle (and someone who can fix machinery when it breaks), administrative support (such as the issuance of pay checks and insurance matters), clean water, medical support, ammunition, and so on. Your job is not to wake up in the morning, shoot the bad guys, and climb back into your bunk for some shut-eye. You will perform a multitude of tasks; few are as exciting as you see in the movies. The details of running a military, no matter how small they may seem, are an important part of the big picture.

So don't join the military because of the image Hollywood has created. The odds are that you could spend many years in the military and never fire your weapon at an enemy. On the other hand, you could be called to serve in a war right after you complete basic training. You won't know until it happens.

Your basic training will prepare you for survival and integrate you into a team capable of awesome power. Remember that when your Drill Sergeant orders you to perform what seems to be a worthless task. He knows what he is doing and has your best interests at heart.

Good luck. You will need it. But you will need less of it if you carefully read this book and prepare yourself in advance.

Sgt. Michael Volkin,
author of the bestseller *The Ultimate Basic Training Guidebook*

Introduction

Joining the U.S. Military is an important decision, and should not be taken lightly. No matter which branch of the military you decide to join, you will have many questions about your decision: questions about jobs, the enlistment process, and of course—basic training. This book will help to answer your questions while guiding you through the two steps required to join the Air Force: enlisting and basic training.

This book is divided into three parts. Part 1, The U. S. Air Force, will give you a basic understanding of what the Air Force is all about and the types of jobs available. Part 2, Joining Made Easy, takes you through the enlistment processes and will provide you with information that will make the process easier and less confusing. Part 3, Welcome to Lackland– Gateway to the Air Force, is where you will find hints, tips, and tactics to surviving Air Force basic training.

While this book will help you survive basic training, more importantly, it will help you succeed before and during basic training. Use it to prepare yourself both physically and mentally for the challenges ahead. You will be glad you did.

Acknowledgments

The first person I need to thank for making this book possible is my recruiter, TSgt Higa. From the very beginning he made my recruiting process as smooth as possible and provided me with all the information I needed to make the important decision of joining the military.

While I was in the process of writing this book, I was deployed to Baghdad, Iraq. I would like to thank every Airman I served with there for their support and encouragement. Special thanks are due SMSgt Coulston, TSgt Aveit, and TSgt Fields for their mentorship and continued guidance; to MSgt Cecil for his words of wisdom; and Hester Mundis for her literary support and advice.

Thanks are also due Michael Volkin, who broke new ground when he wrote his outstanding (and now bestselling) *The Ultimate Basic Training Guidebook: Tips, Tricks, and Tactics for Surviving Boot Camp* (Savas Beatie, 2005). Sgt Volkin offered me invaluable help and graciously penned the Foreword, for which I am thankful.

Finally, I would like to thank my publisher Savas Beatie LLC, and its managing director, Theodore P. Savas, for agreeing to publish my book, and to Sarah Keeney for all her sound marketing advice. It has been a pleasure working with all the people at Savas Beatie.

Nicholas Van Wormer

The photos in the book were taken by Travis Wilton of Wilton Photography (www.wiltonphotography.com), and are used with permission.

Chapter 1

Air Force Overview

This section of *The Ultimate Guide to Air Force Basic Training* will provide you with a basic understanding of what the Air Force is, how it operates, and the types of jobs available within this branch of the service.

Air Force History

The U.S. Air Force, the newest branch of the American military, was created officially in 1947, just two years after World War II ended. Prior to that, the Army Air Corps was responsible for air operations.

After World War II, military officials and politicians realized the importance and effectiveness that air power played during military operations. In order for American air power to meet its full potential, it would have to operate as a separate entity apart from the Army. The National Security Act of 1947 created a separate division of the U.S. Military called The United States Air Force.

Once the Air Force was created, an operating structure had to be established. Here is the current Air Force organization structure:

The Office of the Secretary of the Air Force: The highest positions of the Air Force are found within this office. The SECAF answers directly to the president and the secretary of defense.

Major Commands: These are separate divisions of the Air Force, each with its own mission. During basic training you will be under the Air Education and Training Command (AETC).

Numbered Air Force: These are divisions under Major Commands. Each Numbered Air Force is divided into four levels. (1) Wing: The Wing is responsible for a specific base, operation, or mission. The Wing consists of about 1,000 - 5,000 personnel; (2) Group: A Group has a specific mission under the wing and consists of about 500 - 2,000 personnel; (3) Squadron: A Squadron consists of about 50 - 750 personnel; (4) Flight: The Flight is the lowest level in the Air Force and operates within a given squadron. You will be assigned to a numbered flight during basic training.

Air Force Mission

This was the original mission of the Air Force: *"The Air Force is organized, trained, and equipped primarily for prompt and sustained air offensive and defensive operations."*
This mission statement was developed after World War II, when air battles, "dog fights," and bombing runs were used extensively to defeat an enemy who also had substantial air power to challenge us. With each new war, the Air Force restructured its tactics and priorities. The most drastic change came in 2005, when the Air Force changed its mission statement to reflect present day operations. The changed Air Force mission statement read as follows: *"Deliver sovereign options for the defense of the United States of America and its global interests – to fly and fight in Air, Space and Cyberspace."*
This statement represented the change in technology, including space and cyberspace. However, it wasn't long until the mission statement was changed yet again. In 2008, the Air Force simplified the

statement. The current Air Force mission statement (and the one you will learn in basic training), is: "Fly, fight and win . . . in air, space and cyberspace."

Today's Air Force

With advancement in air technology, the Air Force has expanded its role within the military. One area in which the Air Force has grown is transportation. Modern aircraft can transport supplies and airmen faster than ships, and deliver its cargo directly to a final destination. The Air Force also focuses on aircraft designed for reconnaissance and information gathering. Today, the Air Force inventory consists of more cargo, support, and information gathering aircraft than fighter jets.

As part of its new mission, the Air Force is focused on responding to both combat and non-combat situations within a very short period of time. As a result, a new priority is to have the capability to deploy both supplies and personnel quickly to any part of the world. This requires highly trained personnel prepared to leave on short notice.

Chapter 2

Air Force Personnel and Jobs

When researching different military branches to decide which to join, it is important to know what jobs each branch offers. There is a wide range of jobs available in the Air Force. This chapter includes a list of available jobs within the Air Force (not including officer jobs). Unlike some branches of the military, in the Air Force you do not have to work your way into the job you want. For most jobs, as long as you qualify for it, you can go straight from basic training to your job training school (Technical School), and from there to your first duty station, where you will perform the job you were trained to do.

Job Types

Air Force jobs are broken down into four major categories:

General/Support
Mechanical
Electronics
Administration

General / Support

This category has the most jobs. A few of the jobs in this category include:

Air Traffic Control
Airborne Battle Management
Aircraft Load Master
Airfield Management
Bioenvironmental Engineering
Combat Control (Males Only)
Communications
Dental Assistant
Health Services
Management Fire Protection
Paralegal
Pharmacy
Radio and Television Broadcasting
Security Forces (Air Force Police)
Surgical Services
Tactical Air Control Party
Survival, Evasion, Resistance, and Escape
Weather

Mechanical / Maintenance

Some jobs in this category include:

Aerial Gunner
Air Crew Flight Equipment
Air Traffic Control Maintenance
Biomedical Equipment
Explosive Ordinance Disposal
Flight Engineer
Helicopter Maintenance

Missile and Space Systems Electronics
Munitions Systems
Nuclear Weapons
Pavement and Construction Equipment
Vehicle Operations

Electronics

Some jobs in this category include:

Aircraft Armament Systems
Aircraft Electrical / Environmental Systems
Avionic Systems
Ground Radar Systems
Ground Radio Communications
Missile and Space Systems Maintenance
Network Infrastructure
Satellite, Wideband, and Telemetry Systems
Visual Imagery and Intrusion Detection
Voice Network Systems

Administration

Some jobs in this category include:

Information Management
Logistics Plans
Materiel Management
Personnel
Premier Band
Regional Band
Traffic Management
Vehicle Maintenance Control and Analysis

For a complete list of jobs within this category (with descriptions), I strongly recommend that you speak with an Air Force recruiter and visit www.airforce.com for more information.

As you can see from these lists, most of the jobs in the Air Force do not require extensive combat skills. However, during basic training you will be taught the fundamentals of defending an air base. The Air Force has recently determined that every service member—regardless of his or her job—needs to be equipped and trained to fight in defensive operations.

Chapter 3

Fact or Fiction:
Misconceptions about the Air Force

There are stereotypes for every military branch. When many people think of "Marines," they automatically think of combat, tip-of-the-spear strong, and even mean warriors. When most people think of the Air Force, they think of individuals who are smart, but not necessarily combat-oriented or particularly strong or gung-ho.

I remember the wide variety of conceptions and misconceptions I heard when I told my friends and family I was joining the Air Force. The list below will help you separate fact from fiction.

You need to be extra smart to join the Air Force.

The test score requirements to get into the Air Force and Coast Guard are the highest of all the branches. The education requirements are more stringent than demanded by the other branches. This does not mean that everyone in the Air Force is "smarter" than those who serve in other military branches.

Most people in the Air Force are pilots.

This, of course, is false. Only about four percent (4%) of those who serve in the Air Force are pilots.

Did You Know?

Only about four percent (4%) of those who serve in the Air Force are pilots!

Air Force Basic Training isn't as hard as it is in other military branches.

At one time this was true—which is probably why it received the derogatory nickname "Chair Force." Today, however, Air Force basic training combines physical, mental, and academic exercises into a more challenging experience than at any time in the past, and it is now comparable with Army basic training.

Air Force physical standards are lower than other military branches.

This used to be true. Now, however, the Air Force has increased its physical requirements. This applies to basic training and once you finish basic training and are operational.

The operational Air Force isn't as strict as the Army or Marines.

Every military branch demands discipline and high standards from its members. All military members, regardless of branch, are responsible for following the Uniform Code of Military Justice (UCMJ).

However, as a general rule the Air Force provides more comfort amenities to its members. The Air Force prides itself on making members and their families as comfortable as possible. Another major difference between the Air Force and other military branches is the amount of time members spend away from their families. Currently, the Army and Marines deploy for twelve-plus months, while the average length of an Air Force deployment is only six months.

Most people in the Air Force are officers

This is false. This misconception stems from the thought that smart military members are officers. In fact, a high percentage of enlisted members (non-officers) in the Air Force have four-year college degrees.

You must have a college degree to join the Air Force.

Again, this goes back to the popular misconception that Air Force members are "smarter" than

> **Did You Know?**
>
> You do NOT need to have a college degree to join the Air Force!

other military members. A college degree is only required if you want to enlist as an officer, which is true in all branches. However, as stated previously, many Air Force members have college degrees. Like the other military branches, the Air Force helps its members pursue educational opportunities.

Jobs in the Air Force are all "technical."

Many of the jobs in the Air Force are technically based. However, there are career fields within the Air Force that are more physical and combat-oriented. Security Forces (Air Force Police), Para-rescue, and Combat Control are examples of these types of jobs.

Chapter 4

Air Force Reserve and Air National Guard

This chapter provides basic facts about both the Air Force Reserve and Air National Guard. A high number of active Air Force members did not know about the Air Force Reserve or Air National Guard when they enlisted. Unfortunately, many of them wish they had known about the different options before signing on the dotted line. The Air Force Reserve and Air National Guard each have their own recruiters. If you want to find out more about the Air National Guard, an active Air Force recruiter cannot help you, and visa versa.

Air Force Reserve

Mission: When the Air Force Reserves was created in 1948, it was mainly a stand-by force to be used in times of emergency. Today, it plays a more active role in the Air Force, and provides personnel and equipment for day-to-day operations.

Size: The Air Force Reserve makes up about twenty percent (20%) of the Air Force. Currently, more than 65,000 members serve in the Air Force Reserve. There are more than forty Reserve bases, including one in Alaska and one in Hawaii. Not every state, however, has a Reserve base.

Obligations: The majority of Reserve members are "Traditional Reservists." These members commit to one weekend per month and two weeks per year for training. These members are also obligated to respond when called to active duty by the Federal government. The frequency and length of activation depends on the Reserve unit's mission and the current needs of the Air Force.

Did You Know?
Reservists commit to one weekend of training per month and two weeks per year.

Jobs: Not every Air Force job position is available through the Reserves. Also, not every Reserve job is offered at every Reserve base. The best way to find out what jobs are available is to locate the bases nearest you using a map, and contact those bases directly. Because every Reserve base has a specialty (e.g., air refueling, air transport, and so forth), you may have to travel across the state or to a different state for the job you want. Many Reservists do this because drills are only once a month. For a complete listing of bases, visit www.afreserve.com.

Benefits: Reservists are paid for every drill weekend, two weeks of yearly training they attend, and any other time during which they are activated. Other benefits include educational assistance through the Montgomery GI Bill. The amount and terms of assistance varies, and is determined during the enlistment process.

All Reservists are eligible for the same health care active members receive. While on Reserve status, members must pay for their own healthcare service. If activated, health care is provided by the Air Force.

Reservists can also get auto, home, and life insurance through the military, which is often less expensive than insurance offered by other private providers. Another benefit is the use of military services, such as the Base Exchange/Post Exchange (BX/PX), fitness centers, recreation centers, and so on.

Air National Guard

Mission: The Air National Guard (ANG) has two missions. One is to provide additional support to the Air Force in combat and non-combat missions. The second is to provide its services to the state in times of emergency (e.g., floods, hurricanes, riots, and so on).

Each ANG unit falls under the authority of its state, and can be activated for state emergency by the state governor. At the same time, every guard unit can be activated by the Federal Government to work with the Air Force.

Size: The ANG makes up approximately thirty percent (30%) of the Air Force's combat and combat support forces with more than 100,000 members. There is at least one ANG unit in every state. For a complete list of ANG bases, see www.goang.com.

Obligations: Most ANG members are on drill status, which means they are committed to training one weekend per month, and two weeks out of the year. Usually additional active duty is on a volunteer basis. When either the state or Federal governments need the ANG, its units will ask for volunteers. If not enough members volunteer, then additional members will be selected. There are instances where ANG members are directly activated. The last time this happened was after September 11, 2001.

Jobs: Similar to the Reserves, not every Air Force job is available through the ANG. Likewise, not every ANG base requires every job position. An ANG recruiter will have a list of every job available at the local ANG base. You are not required to be stationed at the closest ANG base, or even one in your state.

Benefits: ANG members are paid for every drill weekend, two weeks of yearly training they attend, and any other time they are activated. They are eligible for the same health benefits as Reservists. Their education benefits include the Montgomery GI Bill, as well as state education benefits. In some states, 100% of tuition is paid. ANG members, like Reservists, can purchase cheaper insurance and use all available military facilities.

Full-Time Jobs: Both the Reserve and ANG have full-time job opportunities. You are eligible for these positions once you have completed basic training and technical school. These positions are highly sought after and are usually filled by members with multiple years of service, special skills, or higher rank. If you are interested in these jobs, ask a Reserve or ANG recruiter what full-time positions are available in your area, and what the eligibility requirements include.

> **Did You Know?**
>
> Basic training is the same for the Reserves and Air National Guard as it is for full-time Air Force members.

Basic training is the same for the Reserve and ANG as it is for full-time Air Force members. No matter which one you join, there is no difference during basic training (and technical school) regarding the training you will receive or how you will be treated.

Chapter 5

How to Talk with a Recruiter

This and the following chapters are designed to help guide you through the process of joining the Air Force, Air National Guard, or Air Force Reserve. These chapters will provide you with the information you need to make it through the enlistment process with the knowledge and the confidence you will need to make the right decisions.

The unknown is what makes basic training so stressful. Not understanding what is happening and why it is happening adds more stress and frustration to an already high-stress situation. This includes the recruiting process. By understanding the process and knowing what to expect, you will empower yourself to make decisions without the stress of the unknown.

The Air Force Recruiter's Job

An Air Force recruiter is not like a used car salesman who tries to sell you something you don't want, don't need, and can't afford. The Air Force recruiter's job is to identify, recruit, and process men and women who meet the standards to attend Air Force Basic Military Training. The Air Force recruiter is not nearly as pressured to meet a quota or the number requirements that some recruiters in other military branches. For this reason alone, the process might seem to take longer than you might otherwise expect.

Contacting a Recruiter

Remember, first impressions are important, and you will make yours during the initial encounter with a recruiter. You want the recruiter to view you as someone who is seriously contemplating the Air Force, not just someone who stopped by on their way to the mall. Recruiters speak to hundreds of people about joining the Air Force, and they will devote more time and energy with someone who is serious about trying to make the right decision to join the Air Force.

Your first step toward meeting with a recruiter should be to initiate a phone call. I do not recommend "popping" into the recruiter's office. If you do this, you run the risk of (a) arriving when the recruiter is out, or; (b) arriving when the recruiter is meeting with someone else, or; (c) giving the impression that you came in on a whim.

When you call, state your first name and that you are interested in speaking with a recruiter about joining the Air Force. At this point you will likely be asked a series of initial screening and informational questions. These basic questions include your name, age, gender, education level, possible medical conditions, and criminal background inquiries. Be absolutely honest and forthright when answering these questions.

These questions will allow the recruiter to determine if you meet the initial requirements to join the Air Force, and will provide the recruiter with your basic background information. Once you have answered all the questions, and are determined to be eligible for the Air Force, your recruiter will set you up with an appointment. Be sure to write down the name of the recruiter with whom you will be meeting.

The recruiting office may tell you to stop by at your convenience without making an appointment. If this happens, simply ask if there is a specific time that would be best to arrive. It is important that you get a specific time and person to meet with. This ensures that you will not

---

Did You Know?

An Air Force recruiter can guarantee you a specific rank upon entry—but you can also be demoted for disciplinary purposes.

---

be waiting too long when you arrive, and that you have the recruiter's full attention when he or she meets with you.

What a Recruiter Can and Cannot Guarantee

The following includes the most common questions people ask about what recruiters can and cannot promise them before they enlist. Keep in mind that some guarantees a recruiter can make are ultimately based upon your own actions. For example, you can be guaranteed a specific rank upon entry, but you can also be demoted for disciplinary purposes.

If you have questions that are not addressed in this book, log onto www.ultimatebasictraining.com. There, you will see a link to Ultimate Basic Training Radio. Call into the show live to talk with host Michael Volkin (author of the bestselling *The Ultimate Basic Training Guidebook: Tips, Tricks, and Tactics for Surviving Boot Camp*) about your basic training questions. He will answer them clearly and fully, and if you ask something he does not know, he will find out and email or call you with his answer.

Here are some common questions about the Air Force recruitment process:

Can a recruiter guarantee me a specific job in the Air Force?

Yes. It is possible for a recruiter to guarantee you a specific job in the Air Force—if you quality. Your ASVAB scores (see Chapter 8), and medical examination (see Chapter 7) are the two major determining factors for job qualification. Once you qualify for a job and it is noted on the enlistment contract, you are guaranteed that specific job. This means that after basic training you will go to technical school for that job you have been guaranteed.

In the Air Force there are a certain number of positions available for every job. Until there is an opening for a job, they will not recruit other individuals for that job. If there are no openings for the job you want, you will have to wait until it becomes available before starting basic training.

You also have the option of going into the Air Force without an assigned job. This is called going in "Open General." During basic training you will be assigned a job according to your ASVAB scores and the needs of the Air Force.

Can a recruiter guarantee when I start basic training?

Yes. Once all of your paperwork is complete and there is an opening for your job, you will be given a start date for basic training.

Can a recruiter guarantee when I will finish basic training?

Yes. Once you are given a start date for basic training, the recruiter can inform you of your graduation date (assuming you pass the standard criteria). If you do not pass the standard criteria, you get "recycled," which means you will start basic training over again. This will affect your date of graduation. (See Chapter 14 for information on being "recycled").

Can a recruiter guarantee where I'll be stationed?

No. You will not know the location of your first duty station until after basic training, and you are attending technical school. The recruiter can provide you with a list of bases in which your job field is located. Air Bases require personnel with specific job skills to complete their specific mission.

Can a recruiter guarantee if and/or how often I will be deployed?

No. No one can tell you if or how often you will be deployed. There are, however, certain jobs that deploy more often than others, such as Security Forces (Military Police).

Can a recruiter guarantee how much I will get paid?

Yes. You will go into the Air Force knowing exactly how much you will be paid. Be aware that your pay during basic training will be less than when you graduate and move on to active duty. The reason for this is because everything that you are issued during basic training comes directly out of your first paychecks. Make sure the recruiter also gives you the information about your allowance amounts. These are monthly allowances for food and housing and will be different depending upon your marital and family status.

Can a recruiter guarantee how long I will be in the Air Force?

Yes. You will know how many years you are enlisting for before you enlist. There will be two different dates on your enlistment paperwork. The first is your active duty enlistment, and the second is your inactive enlistment. If you enlist in the Air Force for four years, and at the end of those four years you decide not to re-enlist, you are thereafter considered a civilian. However, you will still have two years left of inactive service. During this timeframe you can be recalled to service if you are needed.

Can a recruiter guarantee me a specific rank upon entering the Air Force?

Yes. It is possible to go into the Air Force with a higher rank than Airman Basic (the lowest rank in the Air Force). Your enlistment rank depends on the amount of college credits you have and the length of your enlistment and any pre-military training you have (such as Junior

ROTC). Your date of rank (DOR) starts the day you enlist. This means that during basic training, you will get paid according to your rank. Just keep in mind that during basic training you will not be referred to by your rank. Everyone is called "trainee" until you graduate basic training.

Getting Your Questions Answered

Joining any Military branch is a major decision, and the decision to join needs to be made on a personal level. Only you can sign your enlistment

> **Did You Know?**
>
> Make sure you get <u>all</u> of your questions answered to your satisfaction <u>before</u> you sign your enlistment papers!

paperwork. Only you can take your oath of enlistment. No one else can do these things for you. Therefore, it is important you get all of your questions answered to your satisfaction before you enlist.

What to Ask

The most common questions recruiters get asked are about basic training. While this is important, it is not the recruiter's job to explain basic training in detail. Your time with a recruiter will be better spent asking questions about what to expect once you finish basic training, and about your career in the Air Force.

Before you meet with a recruiter, I strongly suggest making a list of questions that are important to you regarding your potential enlistment in the Air Force. Try to think long term. Some of these questions should be specific about any jobs/careers you are interested in pursuing. Your job will determine the location and length of your technical training. You want to have a clear understanding about what you will be doing in the Air Force before you enlist. You should also ask about various health and education benefits. If you have a spouse and children, you will want to get answers regarding relocation and base housing options.

How to Ask

Have these questions ready when you meet with the recruiter. The recruiter will ask if you have any questions, or if there is anything he or she can tell you about the Air Force. Make sure you get each question answered completely to your satisfaction. If the recruiter does not know the answer or is vague, ask if he or she can find out more about it.

As you continue through the recruitment process, you will think of more questions to ask. Simply write down your questions so you don't forget them, and present them to the recruiter during your next meeting. Do not hesitate to ask any questions—no matter how obvious the answer may seem to you.

Bring a Friend

I recommend bringing a family member or friend with you during some, and perhaps all, of your visits with the recruiter. Bring someone you trust and respect, whether it is a parent, spouse, or friend. Sometimes the person you bring may not understand why you want to join the Air Force. Be prepared for skeptical comments or doubts from this person about what the recruiter is telling you. Don't be discouraged by this. Instead, use this skepticism to your advantage. Encourage this person to also ask questions. Often, your friend or family member will ask important questions that would have otherwise gone unasked.

Chapter 6

Prepare Yourself Early

The following issues are often addressed by recruits when it is too late, or are never addressed at all. We will begin by looking at two ways you can save time and stress during the recruiting process by preparing early.

Never Ending Paperwork

During the recruiting process you will be responsible for providing specific records and documents. You can expedite the process by gathering all these records and documents ahead of time. The recruiter will not keep any original copies of these documents. Make extra copies of these documents to take with you to basic training. Even though your personal file with this information is sent with you to basic training, it is still a good idea to have extra copies available—just in case.

Here is a list of documents you will need to provide copies of for the recruiter:

Birth Certificate
Blank Check for Direct Deposit

College Transcripts/Diploma
Dependents' Birth Certificate
Dependents' Social Security Card
Driver's License
High School Diploma
Marriage License
Social Security Card
Spouse's Birth Certificate
Spouse's Driver's License
Spouses Social Security Card

Security Clearance Paperwork

Everyone joining the Air Force is required to complete Standard Form 86. This form is used to gather your background information. If you have a job in the Air Force that requires a higher clearance than Secret, you may have to provide more information. However, this will not be done until you are in technical school or until you have arrived at your first Duty Station.

Because the information you need to provide for Standard Form 86 is so detailed, I would suggest filling out this form as soon as possible. Ask the recruiter for a hard copy of the form so you can take it home for review.

Here is some required information on Standard Form 86 that will take some time to research. (Note: This is not an all-inclusive list of items on Standard Form 86.)

Part 1: Background Information. (This information must go back seven years from the day you complete the form.)

Where You Have Lived?

You will need the information for each residence you lived in during the requested period, and also list a non-relative you knew during that time who can verify this information.

Where You Attended School

For each school you attended within the past three years, you must list someone that you knew during that time who can verify this information.

Your Employment History

Include dates, supervisors name, employer/company name, address, and your job title. (For all periods during which you were unemployed, you will need to list someone who can verify that you were unemployed.)

Three People Who Know You Well

List the names, addresses, and phone numbers of three people you have known well during the last seven years, and how long they have known you.

Relatives

You will need to provide the names, birthdays, and current addresses of the following individuals:

Mother and Stepmother(s)
Father and Stepfather(s)
Foster Parents
Children (including any adopted or foster children)
Stepchildren
Brother(s) and Stepbrother(s) and Half-brother(s)
Sister(s) and Stepsister(s) and Half-sister(s)
Father-in-law(s)
Mother-in-law(s)
Guardian(s)
Spouse(s)

Part 2: Negative History

This section of Standard Form 86 asks questions regarding any drug use, alcohol abuse, job terminations, civil actions taken against you, and financial delinquencies. For any of these sections in which you answer "yes," you will need to provide an explanation. Be completely candid and honest.

Other Important Matters to Keep in Mind

Accuracy

When completing Standard Form 86, it is important to be honest in all your answers—even if you think it would reflect negatively upon you. Lying can be grounds for being discharged from the Air Force.

Anytime you are required to list dates on the form, make sure there are no gaps. For example: When listing where you have lived during the past seven years, the date you put for leaving one residence must match the date you put for moving into the next residence. You do not need to put the exact day; the month and year suffice.

At some point in the recruitment process you will transfer all the information from the hard copy form to a computer. The computer will not process the information if there are any gaps in the dates.

Change Your Physical Habits. Now!

Did You Know?

It is in your best interests to answer every question completely, candidly, and honestly. Lying can be grounds for discharge!

To give yourself a major advantage before you depart for basic training, it is imperative that you start thinking and acting like an Airman as soon as possible. This section will help you begin that journey.

First, start exercising early in the morning. During basic training, your organized physical training sessions will usually be conducted in the morning before breakfast. Therefore, a couple of weeks before you start basic training, make it a habit to get up at 4:30 a.m. so you get used to waking early. Don't just get up and watch television! Get up and follow the workouts described in Chapter 9 of this book. I want to emphasize what a tremendous advantage this will give you over other recruits who wait for basic training before they begin getting into better shape.

Second, change your eating habits. Stop munching on chips and cookies! During basic training there is no snacking. By training your body early to stop snacking, you will help reduce your hunger urges during basic training.

Third, if you smoke or use chewing tobacco, I highly recommend you begin a program to quit immediately. There will be no tobacco products allowed at basic training. (Gone are the days of "Smoke 'em if you got 'em.") It is better to develop a plan to quit on your own terms, rather than on the military's terms. Too many trainees come to basic training and experience a variety of withdrawal symptoms. This only makes the already vigorous and challenging weeks of basic training tougher for you.

Preparing to Leave

If you are leaving in the morning and trying to get your affairs in order the night before, it is too late. There are many things you can do to help make your experience in basic training easier (like reading this book cover to cover, and then reading it again).

Financial Matters

Before you leave for basic training, make sure your financial affairs are in order. How are your bills going to be paid? Do you have enough money in your account to take care of your outstanding obligations until you get a paycheck from Uncle Sam? (Your first paycheck during basic training will be smaller than normal). Some recruits arrange for someone they trust to oversee their financial and personal obligations while they are away. Usually this is a family member, like a parent, brother, or sister. In some cases, you might want to grant someone a Power of Attorney for your financial accounts. This gives a third party of your choice legal authority to handle your affairs during your absence. However, before you take such a step make sure and consult with an attorney first.

Setting up direct payments online is another good way to pay any bills while you are in basic training. Again, make sure you have the money in your account and someone you trust is available to assist you if needed. You are still responsible for any financial obligations while you are in basic training. If you are paying for certain services such as Internet, cable, or phone (none of which you will be using during basic training or technical school), you may consider canceling them. This can save you a considerable amount of money.

Non-Financial Matters

Take a few minutes to write down some of your non-financial responsibilities, like mowing the grass, feeding your pets, and so forth. Make sure you have someone designated to cover each of these matters.

The table on page 28 provides a few examples of non-financial obligations. Be sure to have a back-up plan should your original plan fail. Give this designated person the contact information of your back-up plan individual. Except in case of a true emergency, they will not be able to contact you during basic training. Also, be sure to explain to your employer when you will be leaving (if you are in the Air Force Reserve or Air National Guard), how long you will be gone, and who to contact in case information needs to be relayed to you during basic training.

NON-FINANCIAL RESPONSIBILITIES

Responsibility	Action	Secondary Action
Mow the lawn.	Every Saturday the neighbors will do it.	Neighbors are to call a lawn mowing service.
Feed the pet/take the pet to vet appointments.	A relative or friend can care for the pet.	A pre-designated pet sitter will be called.
Special occasions for loved ones.	Pre-pay for a gift (i.e., flowers) and arrange for a company to deliver the gift on a certain date.	Send a letter or type an e-mail to the company before the occasion.
Miscellaneous chores throughout house (i.e., vacuum, change air filters)	A relative or friend can do the chores.	A pre-designated cleaning service will be called.
Emergencies	Leave local points of contacts posted on the refrigerator and give a wallet-sized card to a neighbor with emergency contact information on it.	

Chapter 7

MEPS: Military Entrance Processing Station

MEPS (Military Entrance Processing Station) is a continuation of the enlistment process. MEPS processes recruits for all military branches. The purpose of MEPS is to determine your eligibility for the Air Force, as well as the specific job you are seeking. Your eligibility is determined by three evaluations: the ASVAB test (see Chapter 8), a medical examination, and a background check.

Traveling to the MEPS

Unless you live near a MEPS, you will travel to the nearest MEPS the day before your appointment and stay in a hotel. The government will cover travel, lodging, and food expenses. Transportation from the hotel to MEPS will also be provided.

Chances are you will be traveling with a group of people going to MEPS. Often, individuals see this time as their last chance to party before going into the military. Do not be drawn into this mindset. What happens at the hotel can be reported to MEPS personnel and have a direct effect on your enlistment process. Go to bed early because you will be waking up around 4:30 a.m.

MEPS Locations by State and Territory

Montgomery, AL	Baltimore, MD	Oklahoma City, OK
Anchorage, AK	Boston, MA	Portland, OR
Phoenix, AZ	Springfield, MA	Harrisburg, PA
Little Rock, AR	Detroit, MI	Pittsburgh, PA
Los Angeles, CA	Lansing, MI	San Juan, PR
Sacramento, CA	Minneapolis, MN	Fort Jackson, SC
San Diego, CA	Jackson, MS	Sioux Falls, SD
San Jose, CA	Kansas City, MO	Knoxville, TN
Denver, CO	St. Louis, MO	Memphis, TN
Jacksonville, FL	Butte, MT	Nashville, TN
Miami, FL	Omaha, NE	Amarillo, TX
Tampa, FL	Fort Dix, NJ	Dallas, TX
Atlanta, GA	Albuquerque, NM	El Paso, TX
Honolulu, HI	Albany, NY	Houston, TX
Boise, ID	Buffalo, NY	San Antonio, TX
Chicago, IL	New York, NY	Salt Lake City, UT
Indianapolis, IN	Syracuse, NY	Fort Lee, VA
Des Moines, IA	Charlotte, NC	Seattle, WA
Louisville, KY	Raleigh, NC	Spokane, WA
New Orleans, LA	Fargo, ND	Beckley, WV
Shreveport, LA	Cleveland, OH	Milwaukee, WI
Portland, ME	Columbus, OH	

Arriving at the MEPS

Think of MEPS as a precursor to BMT. There won't be any Military Training Instructors (MTIs) yelling at you or getting in your face. However, you will do a lot of waiting. They expect you to pay attention and be respectful. It is important to dress both comfortably and appropriately. The following clothes are not allowed at MEPS: sleeveless shirts, tank tops, midriffs, clothing with any objectionable content, open-toed shoes, hats, and headbands.

In addition to these items, do not bring any weapons (including knives of any shape, size, or variety). I would also recommend that you do not wear sunglasses. If you do bring them, make sure to put them away before you enter the building. Because you will do a lot of waiting, I suggest you bring a good book or several magazines. Just make sure that the content is appropriate.

Armed Services Vocational Aptitude Battery (ASVAB)

The ASVAB test will be the first thing you do at MEPS. Once you have completed it, you will go back to the waiting room while the scores are compiled. If you do not score high enough to enter the Air Force, the process stops. You will not continue. You will have to wait thirty days before you can retake the ASVAB. However, if you take the time to study beforehand, you shouldn't have any trouble passing the test. (See Chapter 8 for more information.)

Medical Examination

Everyone who passes the ASVAB will go on to a medical examination. The first part of this exam takes place in a classroom setting, where you will fill out paperwork regarding your medical background and conditions. The military member leading this process will stress that it is important not to leave any medical information out.

You may have heard "horror stories" about people not being able to join the military due to seemingly small medical conditions, such as

---

TIP: Wear clean underwear the day you attend MEPS.

For your sake and for the others around you . . .
I hope you wear clean underwear.

---

a broken bone. Prior medical conditions, such as broken bones and stitches, are not going to keep you from joining the Air Force. If you attend MEPS with a broken bone you can still join the Air Force, but you will have to wait to go to basic until the bone has properly healed.

The next step is the physical examination. The first step in this process is the vision, hearing, and blood pressure test. Going through the MEPS process can be stressful and this, in turn, can raise your blood pressure higher than normal. Remember to relax. At this point you will have completed the ASVAB, and everything else is mostly a waiting game.

There will come a point when the males and females are separated to take the drug and agility tests.

All females will take a pregnancy test. In a group of other males or females, you will remove your clothes (except your underwear) and perform basic motor skills. The examiners are looking for any restrictions in movement. After that, everyone goes into an examination room for a physical examination. For many people this will be the first time they have a complete physical examination. Don't worry, all examinations after the motor skills tests are private.

You will take a drug test during this stage, and this takes the most time. You are not allowed to leave the examination area until you complete the test. Keep this in mind and do not use the restroom directly before the physical examination as you will need to give a urine specimen to complete the drug testing.

Job Search

The next step is the job search. This is when you will meet with an Air Force representative who will have your ASVAB results. The representative will tell you what jobs you qualify for, and even recommend jobs you would do well at based on your ASVAB results. Do not let the recruiter talk you into any job you are not interested in. This is a job that you could be doing for years, and you want to be sure you are happy with your future career. It is important to know what jobs you are interested in and which ones you are not interested in. Be sure to go over the job listings with the recruiter ahead of time.

It is not that easy to change jobs once you have completed all the paperwork. If you do not qualify for the jobs you were interested in doing, do not feel pressured to choose another job right on the spot. Find out from the representative what other jobs you do qualify for and get the information about those jobs. You are not required to make a decision at this time. If you want, you can go back to your recruiter and look into other job options, and then go back to MEPS to finish the process.

Background Check

In addition to any background check paperwork, MEPS will conduct its own background check. This includes taking fingerprints. You will be asked about your background, including medical history and criminal history. You will be asked if you have done any drugs, and if so, when and how often. There isn't a trick to passing this part of the process—except to be honest. Past drug use (that does not show up on your drug test) does not automatically disqualify you from entering the Air Force. However, current or future drug use does.

TIP: Answer all questions honestly. No exceptions.

Past drug use that does not show up when you take your drug test does <u>not</u> automatically disqualify you from going into the Air Force. If you are doing drugs now (or in the near future), you <u>will</u> be disqualified.

Oath of Enlistment

The next step in the process is the oath of enlistment. Friends and family are more than welcome to be present for this ceremony. The oath of enlistment is used for all branches of the military. The oath of enlistment is as follows:

I, (name), do solemnly swear that I will support and defend the Constitution of the United States against all enemies, foreign and domestic; that I will bear true faith and allegiance to the same; and that I will obey the orders of the President of the United States and the orders of the officers appointed over me, according to regulations and the Uniform Code of Military Justice. So help me God.

When enlisting in the Air National Guard you will have an additional line in the oath, stating that you will obey the orders of the Governor of your state.

Enlistment Contract

The final step to enlisting in the Air Force is signing your enlistment papers. Once you sign these papers you are officially enlisted in the United States Air Force. Here is a common question about the enlistment processes: Is it possible to "un-enlist" from the Air Force?

Technically, it is possible to get out of the Air Force after you sign your enlistment contract, and before you leave for basic training. However, it is not easy, and it is not a smart thing to do. Canceling your enlistment can have a long-term effect on future civilian jobs, and it will probably prevent you from joining the Air Force at a later time. Here is the best advice I have for anyone who asks this question:

Everyone has anxieties about joining the military. These anxieties come mostly from not knowing what to expect. The most immediate unknown is basic training. What will it be like? What will I go through? How will I be treated? And so on. That is where the rest of this book comes into play. It will educate you on what you can expect during basic training, and how to handle your basic training experience.

Remember, knowledge is power, and knowledge and power reduce stress and anxiety.

Chapter 8

The All-Important ASVAB

What is the ASVAB?

ASVAB stands for Armed Services Vocational Aptitude Battery. The ASVAB is a multiple choice test used by every branch of the military to determine if you qualify to join a specific branch, and if so, what jobs you qualify for within each branch. The required scores can change, so ask the recruiter for current required scores.

How Does it Work?

The ASVAB is broken into the following eight separate testing categories:

General Science

Arithmetic Reasoning

Word Knowledge

Paragraph Comprehension

Mathematics Knowledge

Electronics Information

Auto and Shop Information

Mechanical Comprehension

The Air Force divides the test results of these eight categories into its four job qualification areas:

Mechanical, Administrative, General, and Electrical.

Mechanical = Mechanical Comprehension, General Science, and Auto and Shop x 2

Administrative = Mathematics Knowledge, Word Knowledge, and Paragraph

General = Word Knowledge, Paragraph Comprehension, and Arithmetic Reasoning

Electrical = Arithmetic Reasoning, Mathematics Knowledge, Electronics Information, and General Science

All jobs in the Air Force fall under one of these categories, and each one has a specific score required in that field to qualify. Because these scores change, ask the recruiter for a current listing.

Each section of the ASVAB is timed separately. The table on page 36 demonstrates how much time is allowed for you to complete each section.

Category Time Limits	
General Science	25 minutes
Arithmetic Reasoning	30 minutes
Word Knowledge	35 minutes
Paragraph Comprehension	15 minutes
Auto and Shop Information	25 minutes
Mathematics Knowledge	25 minutes
Mechanical Comprehension	25 minutes
Electronics Information	20 minutes

When and Where Do I Take the ASVAB?

You will take the ASVAB during your first MEPS visit (see Chapter 7). However, it is possible to take the ASVAB in high school. If you took the ASVAB in high school during your junior or senior year, and it was less than two years ago, you will not have to retake the test at MEPS. In order for the paperwork to get processed properly, be sure to let the recruiter know you took the ASVAB in high school.

How Do I Study for the ASVAB?

Studying for the ASVAB is a lot like studying for the SAT and ACT. There are many books specifically designed to help prepare you for the ASVAB. These books have practice tests, which include questions similar to those on the actual test. In addition to books, there are many websites that have free practice tests for the ASVAB. The key to succeeding at the ASVAB is to take advantage of all the resources available to you, and begin studying well before you take the actual test!

Book Resources

The Armed Services Vocational Aptitude Battery (Kaplan ASVAB 2010 edition)

Master the ASVAB, by Scott A. Ostrow and Therese DeAngelis

ASVAB for Dummies, by Rod Powers and Jennifer Lawler

How to Prepare for the ASVAB with CD-ROM, by Barron's Educational Series

Ace's ASVAB Exambusters Study Cards, by Ace Academics, Inc.

ASVAB Basics, by Ronald Kaprov and Steffi Kaprov

McGraw-Hill's ASVAB with CD-Rom, by Dr. Janet Wall

Web Resources

www.military.com/ASVAB

www.asvabprogram.com

www.testpreppreview.com/asvab

www.4tests.com

www.english-test.net/asvab

Chapter 9

Fit to Fight:
Fitness Preparation for Basic Training

Basic training focuses on building physical fitness and endurance. Your Flight instructor will conduct an organized Physical Readiness Training (PRT) every morning except Sunday. Each PRT session is comprised of three components:

warm-up; conditioning; and cool-down

Generally, you will alternate between running days and push-up/sit-up days. The Air Force measures your physical fitness and endurance by giving you multiple PRT evaluations during the eight weeks of basic training. If you do not pass these evaluations, your MTI will either recycle you back the number of weeks deemed necessary, or you will be enrolled into a fitness improvement program. However, if you do not pass the final PRT evaluation, or fail multiple times, you can be discharged from the Air Force.

The PRT evaluation has three components: two-minute timed push-ups; two-minute timed sit-ups; and one and one-half-mile timed run.

The following chart shows the minimum fitness standards required to graduate BMT.

Minimum Standard (Liberator)		
	Male	Female
1.5 mile run	11.57 minutes	13.56 minutes
Push-ups	45	27
Sit-ups	50	50

You should have no problem meeting the fitness standards by following the exercise program in this chapter for at least eight weeks prior to basic training.

Running Improvement

(Do not follow this exercise regime without speaking to a physician first to determine your fitness and ability to successfully perform without injuring yourself.)

Running is the only fitness category in the PRT evaluation that tests your cardiovascular fitness. Most people have never learned to run properly. However, by learning and applying a few simple techniques, the efficiency of your body movements can increase dramatically. Always try to run with a partner; it is motivating and easier to keep pace with someone running next to you. Just make sure your partner doesn't slow you down. During PRT, you may choose to run with a partner or alone.

The running program in this chapter is to be performed every other day. You will alternate between sprint days and long-run days. By following this program at least eight weeks prior to basic training, you should have no problems passing (or even easily exceeding) the running portion of the PRT evaluation.

Selecting the Proper Running Shoe

The first step in finding the proper running shoe is to determine your foot type. There are three main types of feet: high arch, normal arch, and low arch. To determine which type you are, wet your feet thoroughly and shake off the excess water. Next, step onto a dark and dry surface. I recommend a brown paper bag or piece of smooth wood. The imprint produced will form a shape similar to one of the three shapes shown below:

High Arch   Normal Arch   Low Arch

Foot Shapes

Once you determine which foot type you are, you can shop for the proper running shoe. Don't shop for shoes in the morning; your feet swell slightly when you sleep, which could give you a false assumption of you actual foot size.

If you have highly arched feet, you need a shoe with extra cushioning in the middle area of the shoe. (Army and Air Force Exchange Services [AAFES] tag "C").

If you have a normal foot type, your ankles pronate inward as you step. Therefore, you will need a shoe with average cushioning (AAFES tag "S"). Do not buy a shoe with extra cushioning in one area or extra motion control features.

If you have low arched feet, your ankles pronate inward, but more excessively than the normal foot type. Buy a straight or slightly curved shoe, such as a motion control shoe. (AAFES tag "M"). AAFES tagged shoes can be found at Post Exchanges (PX) and Base Exchanges (BX).

While getting the right shoe for your pre-basic training fitness training is important, you must understand that at basic training you will be issued running shoes. Unless it is determined that you need a different shoe than is provided, you will not be able to wear anything except what is issued.

Stretching

Always gently stretch before you do any physical exercise. The following stretching techniques will help you properly prepare your body for running:

Quadriceps Stretch

Balance yourself against a sturdy object or wall. Grasp your right ankle behind your back with your right hand. Gently pull up with your hand. Figure 1 (right) shows a common mistake many people make when trying to perform this stretch. Be sure to pull at the ankle and not at the toes. Doing this will reduce the chance of an injury. Keep your head up, stand erect, and do not bend over at the waist. Do not bounce. Hold this stretch for a minimum of 30 seconds for each leg.

Figure 1: A common mistake when stretching a quadriceps.

Figure 2: Proper technique for stretching the groin.

Groin Stretch (inner legs)

With your buttocks on the floor place the bottom of your feet together in front of you (Figure 2). Slowly bring your feet as close to your body as possible. Gently grasp your feet and slowly push your knees toward the floor with your elbows. Hold the stretch for a minimum of 30 seconds.

Hamstrings (back of legs)

With your buttocks on the floor, straighten your legs in front of you about 18" apart. Gently reach for the toe on your right foot with your right arm, and hold this for about 30 seconds. When you are finished, repeat this with the left leg, and hold again for about 30 seconds. This simple exercise will stretch the hamstring, but do it gently and slowly, so you do not risk injuring your lower back or pulling a different set of muscles.

Calves (back and bottom of legs)

Lean against a sturdy object/wall with your left leg behind you and your right leg in front bearing most of your weight. Keep the heel of your left foot on the floor with toes pointed forward. Gently move your hips forward toward the wall. The farther forward your hips move (Figure 3), the greater the stretch. Hold for 30 seconds and repeat with the other leg.

Figure 3: Proper calve stretching technique.

Running Techniques

Before you begin any running program you must learn how to run properly. By practicing the various running techniques outlined here, you will greatly improve your efficiency and reduce your risk of injury. Below is a list of quick fix running tips you can use right away with your running program. If you find that these techniques change your stride significantly, then make your changes gradually. These new techniques could put stress on different muscle groups, which could result in an injury until your body adapts to the new running style.

Quick Fix #1

Run with your posture in straight alignment. Your body should be angled forward to where you almost feel like falling over. Be careful not to stick you buttocks out; doing so will create improper balance.

Quick Fix #2

Keep your feet on the ground as little as possible. It is common for people to run heel to toe as their foot strikes the ground. Land on the mid-foot, or forefoot if possible. When you land on your heels, you are placing your body's center of gravity behind you. This forces your body to push harder with every step and wastes energy.

Quick Fix #3

Do not bounce when you run. Use your energy to create horizontal (not vertical) movement. The less vertical movement you have when running, the more energy you can use to propel your body forward.

Quick Fix #4

Your foot should land under your body when it hits the ground, not in front of you. This will ensure better leverage and balance.

Quick Fix # 5

Do not swing your legs back and forth. Instead, when your foot strikes the ground, pull your heel toward your buttocks by contracting the hamstring. This technique creates a shorter leg arch so your legs get in position faster for the next step without any wasted energy.

Quick Fix #6

Resist the temptation to push off with your toes. By contracting your hamstring muscles (as described in quick fix #5) you will save energy for those long runs.

8-Week Running Program

(Use the Appendix tables to record your times for this running program.) Running should be done every other day. Getting sufficient rest is just as important as exercising. Resting allows your body to recuperate and allows your muscles to get stronger after a workout.

This running program can be accomplished regardless of your current fitness level. If you find this program too easy, then add some distance and/or speed to your run. Just make sure that you follow the minimum requirements.

This program gives you eight weeks to get in shape for basic training. If you have more time than eight weeks, then take advantage of it and begin early. If you don't have eight weeks to complete this program, start from the beginning and do what you can. Every little bit helps before you start basic training.

Warm-Up with a Jump Rope

Jumping rope is a great warm-up exercise. It gets your blood flowing, your heart rate up, and your muscles ready for the run. Jumping rope also builds the lower legs muscles that are essential for running. A proper warm-up is outlined in Appendix Table 1 and should be followed before every run. If the jump rope gets tangled and you are forced to restart your movement, add the time you stopped jumping to the time limit you are trying to accomplish.

Initial Assessment

Equipment Needed: Stopwatch and Pedometer

This running program will increase your running speed. Don't ever fall behind in a run during basic training. If you do, your MTI will believe you are unmotivated, and you could lose privileges (such as passes). Before you begin this running program, you need to evaluate your level of fitness with a stopwatch and a pedometer.

A pedometer is a device that attaches to your waistband and calculates how far you have run. A pedometer can be purchased at just about any sports store for a few dollars. If you are running on a standard track, a pedometer is not needed. One complete circle around a standard track is one-quarter (1/4) mile, or 440 yards.

After you have stretched and elevated your heart rate with jump rope exercises, you can begin your assessment. Use your stopwatch to determine how long it takes you to run one mile. One mile equals about four laps around a standard track. Refer back to the chart on page 39 to see the minimum time required to pass the PRT evaluation.

Complete the one-mile run as fast as possible. Log this time (Appendix, Table 2) on all three dotted lines. Be sure to log your time in seconds. For example, an 8:36 minute one-mile run equals 516 seconds. Next, fill in the blanks to determine your "sprint time goal." The .80 will increase your one-mile jog time by 20 percent.

Since this might be your first time running in a while, do whatever it takes to keep running. Absolutely resist the urge to walk. When you alternate running and walking, your body (and your heart) will not be able to maintain a consistent rate. If you absolutely must stop running, then walk briskly. You need to keep you heart rate up to increase your fitness level. Stop if you feel pain. Just remember: push yourself hard on your own terms, or be forced to push yourself on your MTI's terms. Take a one-day rest after the one-mile assessment.

Sprint Day

Initially, run 1/4 of a mile. Be sure to beat the sprint time goal (from Table 2). If you run ¼ of a mile and do not beat the goal, then re-run the 1/4-mile. It might sound tough, but again, better to be disciplined on your own terms than on your MTI's terms. Once you complete a 1/4-mile run, walk briskly for another 1/4 of a mile. You want to keep your heart rate up to increase your stamina. Log your time in Set 1 on Table 3 in the Appendix.

After the 1/4-mile brisk walk, complete a second 1/4 of a mile print, and log this time under Set 2. Again, walk briskly for 1/4 of a mile. Repeat three more times until you have completed all five sets. After completion, be sure to stretch and drink water. After two weeks, fill in the evaluation chart (Appendix, Table 4). Only use the run times in which you surpassed your sprint time goal. If you don't surpass you goal, use the "re-done laps" time instead. Remember, the "re-done laps" are those 1/4-mile laps you had to redo because you failed to surpass your sprint time goal.

Once you complete Tables 3 and 4, continue your running program by completing Tables 5 and 6, Tables 7 and 8, and Tables 9 and 10. With each set of tables completed, run two miles to the best of your ability. Refer back to Table 2 and compare your new two-mile score with the PRT standard. You will be amazed at the improvement. Be sure to keep an accurate log with the table. Charting your progress is important and motivational.

Long-Run Day

On long-run days, your goal is to keep your heart rate up for a measured period of time. If your legs are sore, don't run. Replace running with stretching your legs. Be sure to focus on the running techniques outlined in the beginning of this chapter. Follow Table 11 during long-run days. You are running for a length of time during this session and not necessarily for speed, as you do during sprint days. If you cannot continue running, stop the stopwatch and walk briskly. Continue the stopwatch once you begin running again. Since you are performing the running program every other day, you should alternate between sprint days and long run days.

Push-Up Improvement

The push-up is used by the Air Force to test your upper body strength. There are literally hundreds of exercises you can do to build upper body strength. However, the best way to increase the number of push-ups you can do in two minutes is to actually DO the push-ups.

The push-up program set forth below should be performed every other day, along with the sit-up program. Note: practicing both push-ups and sit-ups too often does not allow for muscle recuperation. Figure 4 shows the proper starting position for a push-up. Notice the back and legs are straight; the head is up and your arms are at shoulder level. Your body should be lowered with the upper arms parallel to the floor keeping your back and legs straight.

Stretching for Push-Ups

The push-up involves numerous upper body muscles, primarily the triceps, chest, and the shoulders. By stretching these muscles before each workout, you will reduce your muscle soreness and your chance of injury. Note: The Air Force PRT program does not include stretching prior to the muscular fitness portion. Instead, it includes warming-up prior to the workout and stretching after the workout is completed. The following stretches can be performed before or after your workout. Additional warm-ups are included later in this chapter.

Triceps (back of arm)

Lift you right arm up over your head with your left hand pushing back on the right triceps just above your right elbow (Figure 5). Hold for 30 seconds and repeat with the left arm. This will also stretch the shoulders.

Figure 4: Push-up starting position

Chest

Position a forearm on the edge of a wall or other stationary object (See Figure 6). Place your feet in line with the wall's edge. Lean out and away from the wall's edge, and hold for a minimum of 30 seconds then repeat with the other arm.

Shoulders

Place your right arm behind your back with your right hand reaching toward your left shoulder (Figure 7). Grab your right wrist with your left hand and pull it gently upward. Hold for 30 seconds, and then repeat with left arm.

Improve Your Push-Up Performance

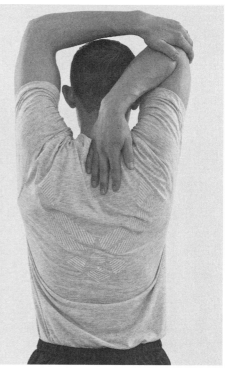

Figure 5: Triceps stretch

This push-up program is designed to be rigorous, regardless of your current fitness level. The more you put into this program, the more you will get out of it. You will be doing both fast and slow push-ups.

Refer to the table on page 60 to see the minimum number of push-ups you must complete to pass the PRT evaluation. Enter that number at the top of table 12. After proper stretching/warming up, see how many push-ups you can do in one minute. Do these push-ups as quickly as possible, but in a controlled manner. Only those push-ups with correct form should be counted. Remember the number of push-ups you just performed. Drop immediately to your knees and continue doing push-ups, but this time put your hands close together (as shown in Figure 8). This type of push-up is a kneeling diamond push-up because your forefingers and thumbs form a diamond shape. These push-ups should be done very slowly—three seconds for the

**Figure 6: Proper
chest stretch**

downward movement, and three seconds for the upward movement. (For many MTIs the regular diamond push-up, those done not on your knees, is a favorite way to motivate trainees).

Keep doing push-ups until you can't continue. When you are done, enter your number in line A and B in Set 1 of Table 12 (enter A for regular push-ups and B for kneeling diamond push-ups). Rest two full minutes and complete another set. Enter those numbers in A and B in Set 2 of Table 12. Complete the third set and stretch afterwards. After three weeks of performing three sets of one minute timed push-ups, complete three weeks of 1:30 minute timed push-ups. For weeks 7 and 8, do three sets of two minute timed push-ups. Perform this workout every other day along with the sit-up program.

Don't be discouraged if by the second or third set your number does not meet the minimum PRT standards. Your muscles will be tired before the sets even start, unlike when you take a PRT evaluation when your muscles are fresh. By the time basic training starts, you will be prepared to meet and exceed the push-up standard.

Figure 7: Proper shoulder stretch

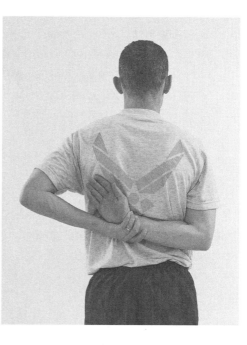

Sit-up Improvement

Figure 9 shows the proper starting position for a sit-up. Notice the legs are bent at a 90-degree angle, the heels are in contact with the floor, and arms are crossed across the chest with the hands resting on the upper chest. During PRT, a partner will be holding your ankles with his hands. Your body should be raised to the position shown in Figure 10. In the vertical position, the base of the neck is above the base of the spine.

During PRT, raising your body to the vertical position and returning it to the lowered position is considered one full repetition. Similar to the push-up, you can save considerable energy during a fitness test by using gravity to let your body return to the lowered

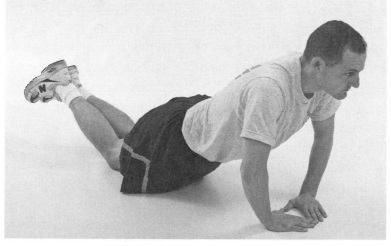

Figure 8: Diamond push-up

position. However, during practice you can build muscular endurance by lowering yourself slowly to the starting position.

This sit-up program is intense, so stop immediately if you feel any abnormal discomfort, rest, and reduce the intensity.

Stretching for Sit-Ups

The sit-up involves the torso and abdominal muscles. Airmen often injure their upper quadriceps (leg muscles) by using the wrong muscles to rise to a vertical position. To thoroughly stretch before a sit-up, perform the stretch described for quadriceps in the running section. Note: sit-ups done improperly can be harmful to the back. The torso extension stretch (Figure 12) will stretch your abdominal muscles and the spine.

To properly perform the torso extension stretch, lie on your stomach and use your forearms to hold your body weight. Relax and slowly raise your upper body, keeping your waist on the floor. Hold for a minimum of 30 seconds. To increase the intensity of the stretch, place the palms of your hands on the floor, instead of your forearms.

Improving Sit-Up Performance

The eight week sit-up program is designed to increase the amount of sit-ups you can do in two minutes. This program is not designed to give you a flat six-pack stomach or melt inches off your waist.

Perform the program on the same day as the push-up program. Before starting, get comfortable by placing a towel under your tailbone or use a soft surface, such as a mat, to lie on. Do not use a bulky surface such as a couch or mattress.

Refer to the table on page 60 to determine the amount of sit-ups you will need to do to pass the PRT evaluation. Enter that number at the top of Table 13. After properly stretching/warming up, see how many sit- ups you can perform in one minute. Do these sit-ups as quickly as possible and with correct form. Be sure to exhale out on the way up. Remember to record the number of the sit-ups you just performed.

Right away you should begin your

Figure 9

Figure 10

abdominal crunches (Figure 13). Once your shoulder blades are off the ground, return to the starting

Figure 11

position. Perform abdominal crunches until you cannot continue. When you are done, enter your number in lines A and B in Set 1 of Table 13 (A for regular sit-ups and B for abdominal crunches). Rest two full minutes and complete another set.

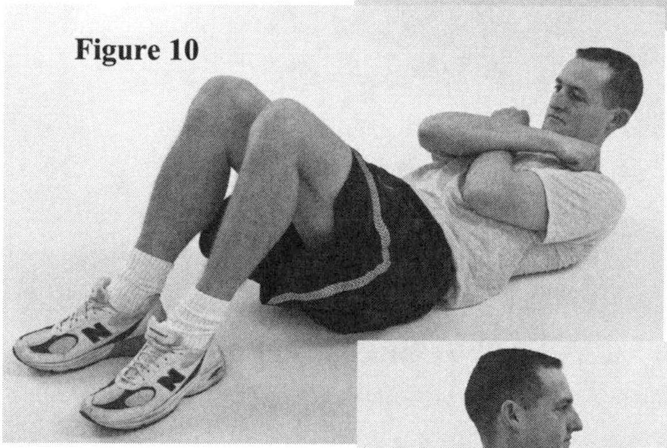

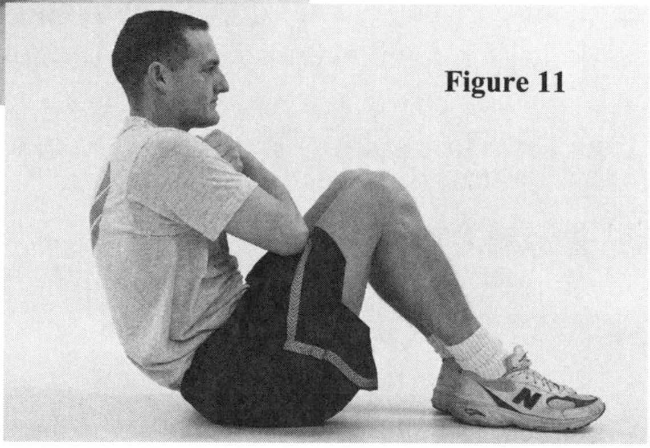

This time, instead of performing abdominal crunches, perform upper-half crunches. The mid-point of the sit-up is the starting position for this exercise (Figure 10). Enter those numbers in lines A and C in Set 2 of Table 13. After three weeks of performing two sets of one minute timed sit-ups, complete three weeks of 1:30 minute timed sit-ups. For weeks 7 and 8, do two sets of 2-minute timed sit-ups. Once this eight-week sit-up improvement program is complete, PRT standards will be easily accomplished.

Figure 12: Torso Extension

Table 14 outlines exactly what you need to accomplish day-by-day, for eight weeks. Use Table 14 as a checklist. If you are unable to workout for a day, do not skip the workout! Instead, use it as a day of rest, and pick up the exercise program the next day where you left off.

Tips for Maximizing Your PRT Score

During PRT, lowering your body and raising it to the starting position is considered one full repetition. Save your energy during your evaluation by using gravity to let your body fall. However, during practice you will want to lower your body in a controlled manner to build muscle.

Avoid muscle failure during PRT when doing the push-ups and sit-ups. When your muscles approach failure, rest for a little while, and then start back up again. Be sure to rest in the authorized position, which will be explained to you before PRT begins.

Sometimes a PRT monitor will not count a repetition for various reasons (i.e., didn't come up high enough on a sit-up, or down far enough on a push-up). When this happens, make a deliberate and obvious attempt to correct your form. Doing this will let the monitor know that you heard the remark and the problem is rectified. Always focus on form. Try not to waste energy on bad repetitions.

Pace your breathing and speed on the running portion of the evaluation. Many trainees get anxious during the run and take off

Figure 13: A proper sit-up for the torso and abdominal muscles

running full speed (or nearly full speed) when the whistle blows. There are many reasons why you should avoid doing this. By starting slow on the run, you will be passing others ½ mile down the road, which is motivational.

Miscellaneous Exercises

Other than push-ups and sit-ups, there are several miscellaneous exercises you will need to know about before arriving at basic training. Some exercises you do in basic training are common knowledge, such as jumping jacks and pull-ups. In basic training, you won't go to a gym and lift weights. Many exercises you do will use your body weight as resistance. This is a good reason to lose weight before basic training starts.

In basic training you will become very familiar with the following exercises. Practice these exercises at home until you are familiar with the form.

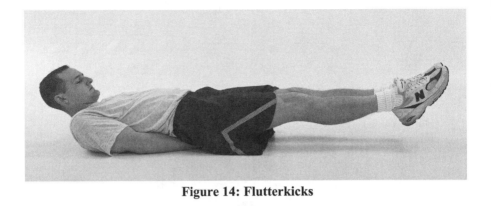

Figure 14: Flutterkicks

Flutterkicks: Strengthens the Stomach

Lie on your back and place your hands under your buttocks. Raise your feet six inches off the ground with your legs very slightly bent, and your head off the ground (Figure 13). This is your starting position. To begin the movement, raise one of your legs about 12 to 16 inches from the floor. As that leg reaches the top, begin returning it to the starting position as you raise the other leg 12 to 16 inches. Repeat this for as long as you can, and once you have finished hold both feet in the starting position for as long as you can hold it there.

Planks: Strengthens the Stomach

Assume the push-up position. Instead of resting on your hands, rest on your forearms (Figure 15). Your back should be straight. Hold this position for one minute. After about twenty seconds you will feel your abdominal muscles getting tight. The further you bring your elbows past your head, the more difficult this exercise will become. (This is another motivational exercise among MTIs).

Leg Lifts: Strengthens the Inner Thighs

Assume the flutterkick starting position. Keep your legs slightly bent with your hands under the buttocks to reduce back strain. Raise

Figure 15: Planks

your legs 12 to 16 inches, and then lower them back down to 6 inches. Immediately spread your feet apart sideways about 24 inches, bring them back together and repeat.

Mountain Climbers: Strengthen the Legs and the Cardiovascular System

Place your hands on the ground approximately three or four feet in front of your feet. Your back should be naturally arched (Figure 16). This is the starting position. Begin the exercise by running in place without moving your hands. Move your knees close to your chest.

Partial Squats: Strengthens the Legs

Standing in a relaxed position with your feet shoulder width apart, bend at the knees until you are in a seated position, keeping your knees in line over your toes. Simultaneously raise your arms straight out in front of you. Return to the starting position, making sure to bring your hands back to your side.

Squat Thrusts

Start in the same position as the partial squats. Squat all the way to the ground placing your hands flat on the ground, about 12 inches in

Figure 16: Mountain Climbers

front of your feet. Once your hands touch the ground, kick both legs out behind you and go into the push-up position, keeping your arms straight, immediately jump back into the squat position, keeping your hands on the ground. Then stand up in the starting position. Repeat.

Additional Stretches

The following stretches are some of the others used after a PRT session as cool down.

Upper Back Stretch

Standing in the neutral position stretch both arms straight out in front. Interlace your fingers with your palms facing away from you. Stretch your arms forward. You will feel the stretch in your upper back.

Abdominal Stretch

Standing in the neutral position, interlace your fingers just like in the upper back stretch. This time raise your hands straight above your head. Stretch your arms up as far as you can. Keep your feet flat on the ground.

Chest Stretch

Standing in the neutral position, interlace your fingers behind your back with you palms facing you. Raise your hands as high as you can while at the same time stretching your chest.

Cat Stretch (or Bulldog Stretch if you are in the 326 TR Squadron)

Get on the ground on your hands and knees. Arch your back and hold for 5 to 10 seconds. Relax back down into the starting position.

Back Stretch

Lie on your back and bring your knees up to your chest. Wrap your arms around your knees and hold them there.

Hamstring Stretch

Lie flat on your back. Raise you left leg into the air keeping it straight. With both hands, hold your left leg just below the knee joint and slowly pull.

While the table on page 60 shows the minimum standards to pass your PRT evaluation, it also shows the Air Force's two other levels of fitness standards.

AIR FORCE FITNESS LEVELS						
	Liberator		Thunderbolt		Warhawk	
	Male	Female	Male	Female	Male	Female
1.5 mile	11:57	13:56	9:30	12:00	8:55	10:55
Push-ups	45	27	55	32	65	40
Sit-ups	50	50	60	55	70	60
Pull-ups	0	0	5	2	10	5

Notice that pull-ups are counted to meet the Thunderbolt and Warhawk fitness levels, but they are not required to pass the evaluation. Essentially, the two additional fitness levels are added incentive to exceed the minimum requirements. By achieving the Thunderbolt or the Warhawk fitness level, trainees become eligible for extra day passes, town passes, and Honor Graduate recognition—"eligible" being the key word. Meeting these physical fitness standards does not guarantee these things. There are many other elements that are considered, such as inspections, written tests, and general behavior.

Chapter 10

Packing for BMT:
Helpful Tips on What to Bring

The trick to packing for basic training is to bring everything you will need—and no more. A single carry-on suitcase is plenty for the amount of clothes you will want or need. Do not bring any luggage that will have to be checked on the plane. If you check any luggage, you will have to make a detour to the baggage claim when you arrive, and you want to be able to get off the plane and go straight to the United Service Organization (USO).

Clothing Items

Bring enough clothes to last about four days. You will not have a chance to wash your civilian clothes. Be sure to bring enough so that you don't start to smell. MTIs will pick out smelly trainees right away. Males will be issued underwear as soon as you arrive at basic training. Males will be required to wear briefs during basic training unless you can get a waiver allowing you to wear boxers. Females must provide their own undergarments.

Do not bring any civilian clothes that will draw attention to yourself. This includes anything with a military logo on it. One of the first things an MTI looks for with a new Flight is someone wearing an Air Force shirt or camouflage pants. Wearing either of these is an instant invitation for special attention. You do not want special attention during basic training! Instead, wear neutral-colored clothes and avoid any and all logos.

Packing List (Everyone)

Plane ticket
Orders (Bring several copies.)
All MEPS documents
Copies: Birth Certificate, College Transcripts, Marriage License
Driver's License
Social Security Card
One pair of comfortable shoes (no sandals or open-toed shoes)
Eyeglasses (no contact lenses)
Toothbrush with case
Toothpaste
Dental floss
Disposable razors or electric razor
Shaving cream. (Do not bring shaving gel. It will leak in your wall locker.)
Deodorant (stick type, that won't leave marks on your clothes)
Shower shoes (all-black with no logo)
Shampoo/conditioner in one bottle. (For males, a small bottle is plenty. Also, make sure the shampoo is clear or white. This is explained in Chapter 16.)
Soap with case
Washcloth and towel
Calling cards
Stamps
Stationery
Sunscreen
A small notebook
Black pens
Cell phone (You are permitted to bring a cell phone with you to basic training. You can use it on the way to basic training, and you can

use it upon graduating. However, make sure you turn it off and put it away prior to arriving at Lackland!)

Packing List for Women (in addition to the above list)

Panties (cotton)
Bras/sports bras
Sanitary napkins/products
Nylons/panty hose
Brush or comb
Hair bands and bobby pins

Every item on this list can be purchased during basic training. Your flight will go to the BX (Base Exchange) to purchase these and more items. Below is a list of additional items that you should purchase at the BX. You do not need to bring these items with you:

Sewing kit
Shirt garters
Nail trimming kit. (The scissors work well for cutting strings off of uniforms.)
Foot powder
Baby wipes (for dorm details and cleaning yourself when there is no time for showers).
Hand sanitizer (at least two bottles)
Q-tips
Scented body spray (Use this for spraying your wall locker, and it works well for getting scuff marks off the floor.)

What Not to Bring to Basic Training

Weapons (including pocket knives and multi-tools)
Playing cards
Dice
Cigarettes or chewing tobacco

Lighter
Over-the-counter drugs
Cough drops. (You will be given these if you need them.)
Alcohol
Aerosol cans (deodorant, hair spray, etc.)
Pornographic material
Locks (you will be provided with these)

Packing

Use this chapter as your starting packing list when you are getting ready to leave for basic training. Start packing two or three days before you leave. This will give you time to remember anything you may have forgotten.

Chapter 11

Military Training Instructors: The Mental Game

In the Air Force, "Drill Sergeants" are called Military Training Instructors (MTIs), or Training Instructors (TIs) for short. However, at no time during training will you call any instructor by these titles. In fact, you will call your instructors and all other military personnel "Sir" or "Ma'am"—regardless of rank.

MTIs wear a campaign hat similar to those worn by Drill Instructors of other military branches. The most obvious difference is that the MTI hats are blue.

How to Play the Basic Training "Game"

First and foremost, you must understand that basic training is as much a mind game as it is a physical challenge. Second, always remember not to take anything personally. Finally, you need to know why MTIs behave and act like they do.

MTIs have the job of turning raw civilians into airmen. When MTIs receive a flight of 50 or so individuals, not only are they responsible for the safety, morale, and training of each individual, they are also responsible for turning those 50 individuals into a unified group that can successfully work together toward a common goal. This is a lot to accomplish in only eight weeks.

You may have heard the saying "break them down to build them up." This is essentially the method they use to achieve these goals. Keep in mind that each individual comes from a different place, and brings with him or her a different background and different life experiences. The first thing MTIs need to do is get everyone on the same page. This is done by removing personal prejudices and self-pride. Only then will it be possible for an MTI to build up airmen into a unified team. Trainees who have problems with this process often say "I have a right to . . . " or "They can't make me . . ." Do NOT be one of the people who say or even think such things. Those who do are letting their egos get in the way of training. They are taking these actions personally—which only makes basic training more stressful for themselves and everyone around them.

MTIs will yell, belittle, and ask questions that seem to have no right answer. Keep in mind they will not hit you, push you, or spit on you (although some saliva does shoot out when they yell in your face!). The way to respond to any of these things is with confidence and respect. When an MTI is getting in your face, DO NOT look away. Look the MTI in the face and if you are asked a question, answer it as honestly and directly as possible. Do not attempt to come up with the "right" answer. The right answer is the honest answer, even if you do not know the answer. It is better to tell the MTI that you do not know the answer then to try and make one up. Regardless of how you answer, answer with confidence, even if you don't know the answer. Many times it does not matter what you answer because they will find something wrong with it regardless of what you say. An answer that is wrong and sounds confident, however, is almost as good as an answer this is right but spoken with no confidence and a soft, tentative voice.

Another common training tactic you will encounter are tasks with time limits that are impossible to meet. These will include having the entire flight getting changed out of Physical Readiness Training (PRT) gear and into Airman Battle Uniform (ABU) in five minutes. At the beginning of training the reaction to this type of order is panic and chaos. As time goes on, you will learn how to work under pressure and work well together.

Play as a Team

In order to succeed at basic training, you must learn to work well with others. Basic training is a process designed to require trainees to work together. While you may not be assigned "battle buddies" in your flight, everyone is expected to be a good "wingman." Basically this means helping each other and looking out for your fellow trainees (whether you like them or not).

This "Play as a Team" philosophy even applies to the everyday actives like making your bed in the morning. Instead of everyone rushing to make his or her own bed, and make it right, it goes a lot faster and the beds are made better when two trainees work together to make each other's bed.

Chapter 12

Arriving in San Antonio: The Beginning of Zero Week

As soon as you touchdown at the San Antonio airport, and the Flight Attendant announces that cell phone use is permitted, call home. (As stated in Chapter 10, you are allowed to bring cell phones to basic training.) The reason for calling home now is because you don't know exactly when you will have a chance to later. So call and let your family know you made it safely to San Antonio. If you don't bring your cell phone, there are payphones located near the USO or you can borrow someone else's phone.

Once you deplane, find your way to the USO. There are signs to show you the way. In the San Antonio airport, the USO is located in the northern most part of Terminal 2. You may or may not run into military personnel when you exit the plane or even along your way to the USO. If you do, they will tell you how to get to the USO. Don't worry, Basic Training hasn't started yet and they won't yell at you in the middle of the airport. Volunteer military veterans operate the USO and they will be extremely nice to you, so make sure you are respectful to them in return. The USO will provide you with free drinks, snacks, soft sofas, and Large Screen TVs while you wait for the bus ride to Lackland AFB. Relax and drink something with caffeine—you have a long night ahead of you.

HINT: During your wait in the USO, chances are there will be military members waiting there as well. Avoid talking with them. They know why you are there and how you are feeling. So to "help you out," they will tell you their own horror stories of basic training, which are almost always exaggerated or, in some cases, complete untrue.

Bus Ride #1

The bus ride from the Airport to Lackland AFB is a relaxing trip. Not like the movie Forrest Gump where the driver yells and calls you names. That comes later. The driver is a civilian whose job is to drive the bus, not train trainees. Feel free to talk on the bus, find out where everyone is from and so on. Once you arrive at the Lackland AFB front gate the natural instinct is to stop talking, which is a good idea at this point. The bus stops and you can see military personnel outside waiting for you. As soon as the bus doors open you can expect a lot of yelling and people telling you to do things faster than humanly possible. Welcome, you have arrived and the unprepared trainees are lost and scared, but not you. You have read this book so you know what will happen next and what is expected of you.

Beginning of Zero Week

Why is it called Zero Week? Because the Air Force doesn't count it as a week of training. So when you are told that basic training is eight weeks long that does not include Zero Week.

What is Zero Week? This is the week (usually three to four days) that you are processed into the Air Force system.

The Air Force doesn't waste any time, and the second you step off the bus the processing begins. The first day is the easiest. All you have to do on the first day is follow instructions, which consist of telling you where to stand, sit, and not to talk. If you follow the information in Chapter 10, there is no reason why anyone would pick you out of the crowd to be made an example of. Leave that to the person who wears the BDU pants. You will quickly be brought inside, handed some books and told to sit, read and be quiet. You will sit and read, and sit and read some more. This can last several hours. You are allowed to use the restroom and get water. Why the long wait? More than likely you are waiting for the rest of the Trainees to arrive. Until everyone arrives who is assigned to specific Squadrons, no one leaves.

During this time you will see people in uniform who do not have any rank. (no stripes on their sleeves). These people will be telling you what to do, but not as effectively as those who have blue stripes. That is because, believe it or not, they are trainees just like you. The only difference is that they are further along in training. Do what they say, but don't be afraid of them. Finally, you will be told to get in a line in the hall. You will go into a room with a group of men or women (during basic training the Air Force is very conscience of male and female modesty issues) where you will be told to strip down to your skivvies. Don't forget your underwear or this part could be very embarrassing for you. Once you are all undressed, one at a time you will stand in a machine that will measure you for your uniforms using high-tech laser technology. Therefore, you can count on the measurements to be off one way or another.

Bus Ride #2

Eventually you will get back on a bus and head to your dorms. For most trainees the first night is something of a blur. It consists of finding a bunk, going to sleep, being woken up a couple of times in the night to stand at "attention," going back to bed and then waking up in the morning wondering if it is alright to get out of bed and go to the bathroom. Usually it is at this time where you will meet your Military Training Instructor (MTI or TI).

Your New Home

You are now in your dorm and with the members of your basic training class, which the Air Force calls a Flight. Your class will have a number and be referred to as Flight 010, or Flight 299, whatever your number might be. Within your Flight you are all numbered. Tip: remember what number you are. There can be more than one of the same numbers. This happens when you have Air Force Reserves or Air National Guard members in the flight. They are numbered separately and will have additional letters added to their numbers. These numbers are used mainly during flight appointment.

Your dorm consists of two separate sleeping quarters called bays: A bay and B bay. Between these two bays is the Flight Office, where your MTI does paperwork and may even sleep at night. There is also the restroom, called the latrine. The shower consists of a single room with multiple showerheads. The other room in your dorm is called the dayroom. This room is used for group instruction and anytime your MTI wants you all out of the bays, for example, during locker inspections (more on that in Chapter 16). In the dayroom you will notice padded chairs lined up along the walls. These are not for you to sit in or use, same goes for the TV.

Bag Dumps

One of the first group activities to take place in the dorms is the bag dump. This is where all of your personal belongings are dumped out and gone through by an MTI. If you follow the suggestions in Chapter 10 you should have no problems. This doesn't mean they won't give you a hard time. They'll do that no matter what you bring. Once all unauthorized objects (called contraband) have been disposed of, all of your items will be returned to your bag. TIs will take your cell phone and lock it in the Flight Office. They will be given back to you to use during designated times. Your bag is tagged and locked away once you have been issued your uniforms. You will not be able to get to your bag after that until the last week.

The Basic Training Dining Experience

Eating at basic training is an event in and of itself. At first you may dread these fast, crazy, stressful few minutes that happen three times a day. But eventually you come to look forward to these scheduled face stuffing moments, if only as a means of counting down the time until graduation. Even after graduating basic training, you will find yourself eating extremely fast, just out of habit.

Here are the fundamental mechanics of meal times. Once your Flight is called into the chow hall:

1. You sign-in.

2. You walk in a line and get your silverware and tray.

3. You sidestep (right foot, left foot, right foot, left foot) down the line.

4. You keep your tray on the ledge and both hands on the tray.

5. You make sure to keep you head and eyes straightforward. Do not look around.

6. You get your food and three drinks as fast as you can.

7. You go to the table you're directed to.

8. Sit when there are three other Trainees standing at the table (do not put the tray on the table until the other three Trainees are there).

9. Sit and eat.

10. When you are done, flip your empty glasses upside-down on the tray.

11. When you're told, get up and take your tray to the tray counter.

12. Leave.

No problem, right? Anyone could do that. Of course what fun would it be without half-a dozen MTIs bouncing around from table to table, and on special occasions even on tables. The fact is, during your first few times at the chow hall, the MTIs are going to do what they can to confuse, and generally stress you out. Not that they won't do that at other times. However, the chow hall is a good environment to play these mind games. Why the chow hall? The chow hall is one of the first times you are given a list of simple instructions to follow while doing something safe—eating. It isn't uncommon for some trainees to get so worked up during their first meal that they lose it. By "it" I mean their meal, and often all over the table where others are eating. If you can, avoid doing this. MTIs won't be sympathetic and it will only give them something else to yell at you about.

The Snake Pit

The Snake Pit is simply a table where the head MTIs (Blue Ropes) and the other MTIs sit and eat. The problem is that you will have to pass by it in order to sit at your table. An additional dilemma is that they can call you out of the line and drill you. What they drill you on depends on what week of training you are in. They may simply have you dump out your portfolio (which you will be issued to carry with you at all times) to make sure you do not have any "unauthorized" items in it. Because you will have more information to be tested on as the weeks go on, your chances of getting called to the Snake Pit increase with each passing day. The best advice for handling the Snake Pit is don't get called over to it. How do you that? There is no sure way to avoid it, but for the most part the MTIs are looking for people that either (a) make eye contact with them, (b) can't seem to follow the chow hall rules, or (c) just look like a goofball. So if you don't do any of these things, you have better odds of being able to sit, eat, and get out!

HINT: Even if your MTI allows you to drink soda or milk (which is unlikely during the first couple of weeks) don't do it. Soda will dehydrate you, and milk will not absorb well in your stomach because of the stressful environment. Instead, I highly recommend that you stick to a sports drink and water. If you start getting leg cramps from a lack of milk, eat bananas. Bananas are an excellent source of potassium, which helps prevent cramping.

Haircuts

Men are required to get haircuts, and women are not allowed to. Getting a haircut seems to be a symbol of transitioning from a civilian to an airman. Your hair is one of the first things taken from you to make everyone look the same. The Air Force barbers are all civilians, but they don't care about how you are doing or look, so don't tell them or ask. Be prepared for a rough cut; occasionally they get a little too close. Here are a couple of tips to keep in mind about your hair:

1) Before coming to basic training, don't color it, don't get a Mohawk, and don't get a military-style cut!

2) Don't grow facial hair before coming to basic training. Any one of these things will draw unwanted attention to yourself.

First Clothing Issue

This is another milestone to feeling like you're in the Air Force. Your first clothing issue is done in assembly line fashion without a lot of attention to personal fit. Remember the high-tech laser-measuring machine? It is now put to use. You are given a printout of all your measurements that will be used to issue your ABUs. It seems normal for the measurements to run large. You will try on your uniforms to see if they fit reasonably well. This is the time to make sure you get clothes that don't make you look like Bozo the Clown. Once again, many of the people working at the clothing issue are other Trainees further along in training than you are. They are not experts on what fits and what doesn't (and they don't really care that much), so don't be afraid to say (politely) that something is too big or too small.

BDU versus ABU

In the fall of 2007, airmen in basic training were issued ABUs (Airman Battle Uniforms) instead of BDUs (Battle Dress Uniforms). ABUs eliminate a lot of the upkeep and care, which the BDUs required. They do not need to be ironed and do not require dry-cleaning. The boots are suede, so they do not need to be polished.

In addition, they are also used in place of DCUs (Desert Camouflage Uniforms), which eliminates the need for additional uniforms.

Shots . . . and More Shots

This process is quick and easy, but not always painless. It is easy because all you have to do is your best imitation of a pincushion. The majority of the shots will be in your arms with the exception of one in the rear. There is no use making a fuss over any of the shots. You will get no sympathy. Simply get your shots and move on.

The Drug Test

This pee-in-the-cup test takes a long time because half of your Flight will freeze when it's time to contribute. While waiting, you'll be asked if you're ready. Unless you are 100% sure you can "take the test," don't enter the latrine. Instead, wait in line and drink water. The people administering the test get upset if you fail to produce a sample.

The First Fitness Test

This first test measures your physical improvement through basic training, evaluated on running, push-ups, and sit-ups. The Air Force suggests that you are able to do the following for the first fitness test.

	1.5 mile run	Push-ups	Sit-ups
Males	13:45 minutes	34	38
Females	16:01 minutes	21	38

If you meet these standards, great! If you do not meet them, you may be required to attend Remedial PRT (Physical Readiness Training) during basic training. Remedial PRT will cut into the little time you have to prepare your wall locker for inspections. I do not advise excelling well beyond these standards during your first test. All future fitness tests are measured against the first test, so if you try your hardest at this time, you will be reducing your percentage of improvement later when they measure you again. If you are not able to produce the same stellar results, then you will not be showing improvement. Remember, improvement is what your MTI is looking for. (See Chapter 9 to ensure you are prepared for the PRT test).

The All-Important Reporting Statement

The reporting statement is how you will always start a "conversation" with any MTI. Here it is: *"Sir (or Ma'am), Trainee Smith reports as ordered."* As short and simple as this seems, new trainees always mix it up. Practice ahead of time, but don't use it until they teach it to you. Otherwise, you will be asking for special attention by doing anything before your MTI teaches it to you. People who have had some pre-military training often make this mistake. Keep your knowledge to yourself until you're told how and when to use it.

The End of Zero Week

Ironically, this week is considered by many airmen to be the hardest week of basic training. Why?

- Because everything is new.
- MTIs are focusing on breaking you down as a civilian and getting you ready for the military lifestyle.
- No day is the same. Nothing seems predictable. You will find it impossible to settle into any kind of reasonable routine.

What can you do to make it easier for yourself? (This goes for every week of basic training.) Follow these tips:

1. Remember that much of basic training is a mind game.
2. Stay out of Flight bickering and arguments.
3. Don't listen to other Trainees! They know less than you!
4. Do what you're told, when you're told, and how you're told.

You are now ready to move on to the "official" first week of training.

Chapter 13

Make the Most of Your Meals

During basic training, if you get more than three minutes to eat your meal, consider yourself lucky. Many trainees go to bed hungry at night. But it doesn't have to be this way. Your food consumption can increase dramatically by following the tips in this chapter.

Eat Smart

If given the option, always choose to eat rice. Always eat it first, along with the main course. Rice grains expand in your stomach and give you a full feeling. Rice (especially brown rice) is packed with the healthy carbohydrates your body needs to fuel your physical training.

Think S-A-N-D-W-I-C-H

Whenever possible, make a sandwich out of your food. Let's suppose your meal is chili macaroni with mashed potatoes and peas. Instead of trying to cram little macaronis on your fork, spread the macaroni on bread with the potatoes and peas. Air Force-style mashed potatoes can glue any two foods together. Add another bread slice and voila!—you have a full-meal sandwich and will be done eating in seconds. (Don't worry about it tasting odd; you won't even have time to taste it!).

Will you look a bit odd doing this? Yes. Do you care? No! Some trainees may even laugh at you (except for those who were smart enough to buy and read this book). Just smile in return (as long as there isn't an MTI around), because you will be leaving the chow hall with a full stomach. After you have eaten your fill and time runs out, many others will be halfway through and therefore . . . still hungry.

You will also be surprised how much quicker it is to eat with your hands than it is with your utensils.

Water . . . Water . . . WATER!

You are required to drink three glasses of water at each meal. However, don't save them all until you are finished eating. Many trainees choke trying to eat too much food, too fast. During basic training, you will almost certainly witness an MTI performing the abdominal thrust on a choking trainee. This is less likely to happen to you if you drink water throughout your meal. Water lubricates your throat and allows the food to slide down easier.

Look for These Foods

Choose meals high in protein, such as beef, fish, and chicken. Protein is a building block for muscles and makes you feel full.

Avoid eating sugar. Sugar is filled with empty calories and will leave you feeling hungry.

A Few Other Miscellaneous Meal Tips

1. The closer your mouth is to your plate, the faster you will eat. It will also keep you from looking around, or even talking. Two popular reasons for MTIs to yell at trainees during meals. You may look like a pig, but you will be a pig with a full stomach.

2. Avoid adding salt, pepper, or sauces to your food. Sauces have little, if any nutritional value and they get on your uniform when you

eat fast. Squeezing on ketchup or steak sauce only wastes precious time. Remember: you are not there to taste your food; you are there to sit, eat, and get out! You will hear this said at every meal.

3. Don't touch or even look at the deserts in the display case. Yes, you are allowed to eat anything that is in the chow hall, but eating deserts is a bad idea. Why? There are two good reasons.

Reason #1: It isn't healthy, and it will have a negative effect on your physical performance;

Reason #2: Every MTI in the chow hall will swarm to you like a moth to a flame when they see you trying to eat desert.

Let some other trainee get "smoked." You read this book. You know better.

Chapter 14

Week 1: How to Survive the Beginning of Training

Your MTI will assign dorm details to the Flight. Dorm details are chores you are responsible for completing for the remainder of basic training. The dorm detail you are assigned to can have a huge effect on your basic training experience. The trick is to understand how your MTI assigns details and what these details include.

As part of the mind game, your MTI won't come right out and tell you that he is assigning details. Instead he will ask questions like this: "Does anyone do their own laundry, or does your mommy do it for you?" The few trainees who are foolish enough to raise their hands to indicate that they do their own laundry are assigned to the laundry crew and are now responsible for doing everyone's laundry for the remainder of basic training.

Below is a list of some detail assignments, what they entail, and how often they need to be done:

Dorm Chief: This position can be selected during the in-processing stage. However, this can and often does change during basic training. This position is the most demanding and time consuming detail assignment. The individual in this position is responsible for the rest of the Flight not only during dorm details, but anytime the MTI is not around. MTIs look for individuals who naturally take charge of others for this position.

Element Leaders (four): There are four Element Leaders, one for each element (Flight formation is divided into four rows, and these rows are called "elements"). The role of the Element Leaders is to support the Dorm Chief by taking responsibility for their Elements. The individuals in these positions are also responsible for the members in their Element throughout the day.

Entry Control Monitor: Directly following Dorm Chief and Element Leader, Entry Control Monitor can be a very stressful position. This individual (or sometimes two individuals) is responsible for assigning trainees to Entry Control Duty. (EC Duty is explained later in this chapter.) When a trainee makes a mistake during EC Duty—it happens often—the EC Monitor is responsible. Not only does this person get a lot of attention from MTIs, he will also have the challenge of assigning fellow trainees to an unpopular task.

Latrine Crew (Latrine Queen): This is another assignment that receives a lot of attention from MTIs. Because it is hard to keep the latrine spotless at all times, it is a focal point during scheduled and "unscheduled" inspections. Tip: For male Flights, don't let anyone use the urinals. They get dirty fast and are harder to clean. Everyone should use the toilet bowls and you may even make the rule that everyone must sit on the toilet for every use.

> *Tip: If your MTI asks, "Does anyone like to bowl?"—don't raise your hand!*
>
> Now you know what he is really asking . . .

Laundry Crew: Not only is this crew responsible for doing everyone's laundry, but they also have the task of getting everyone's laundry back to the proper owner. There are scheduled laundry times in the day, but they never seem to be long enough to get everything done. While everyone else is studying or working on their wall lockers, the Laundry Crew is busy washing clothes.

Tip: Come up with a system for distributing clean laundry where everyone must pick their laundry up, rather than running around the dorm to deliver all of it.

Flight Office Technician (House Mouse): The duties for this assignment vary from Flight to Flight. Some MTIs simply have the House Mouse keep the Flight office clean, while others will have this individual do simple paperwork in the office to include keeping track of trainee appointments.

Chow Runner: The Chow Runner goes into the dining hall to announce that the Flight is prepared to enter. Once that has been done, the Chow Runner directs the rest of the Flight where to sit. While the rest of the Flight is focused on getting food, sitting down, eating ,and getting out, the Chow Runner has to focus on making sure everyone is sitting in the right spot at the right time, while multiple MTIs watch.

Road Guards: This is a continual duty. Whenever the Flight marches from one location to another, the Road Guards must be ready. The duty of Road Guards is to stop traffic in the roads to let the Flight cross safely. In order to do this, the Road Guards must run ahead of the Flight to stop traffic, and then run to catch up with the Flight once everyone has crossed the road. This duty is usually given to individuals who need to lose the most weight.

Chapel Guide: The task of this position is to escort new Flights to and from chapel services on Sundays. The downside to this assignment is it eliminates any "free time" on Sundays to study or work on your wall locker. Because this assignment is only on Sundays, there is a good chance that this individual will be assigned to another crew for details.

Other detail assignments include: Bed Aligner; Shoe Aligner; Hall Crew; Floor Crew; Utility Room Crew and Stairwell Crew. While these are just as important as the ones listed above, they are only done during allotted detail times, alleviating any extra pressure that comes from other detail assignments.

While there is no way of getting out of details or of picking what detail you are assigned to, by not volunteering information about what you are capable of performing, you stand a greater chance of not being assigned to those details that take more time.

Regardless, there are three keys to succeeding at any detail to which you are assigned:

1. When given an assignment, don't show any sign of relief or displeasure. Your MTI will either switch you to one he thinks you won't like, or one that is even more undesirable.

2. Take your assignment seriously. Even if you are simply aligning beds, make sure it is done right every time. (The Shoe Aligner in my Flight was recycled because he didn't think it would be noticed if he did or didn't align everyone's shoes.)

Tip: If you are assigned as a Chapel Guide, be careful about socializing too much with the Flights you are escorting—especially if they are of the opposite gender.

3. Understand that everyone else has a job equally important as yours. Work with and around the other trainees to get all the jobs done. Remember, you are all on the same team, and teamwork is the key to success.

Succeeding Where Most Trainees Fail: Entry Control Duty

There will come a time early on in training where you will be assigned to Entry Control Duty. What is Entry Control, or EC Duty? Simply put, the job of the trainee on EC Duty is to allow authorized people into the dorm and keep unauthorized people out of the dorm. To make this job even easier than it sounds, there are typed instructions on the door, which you simply read word for word before allowing or denying entry. In addition, there is a list next to the door with the names of the people allowed to enter the dorm. So why do so many trainees make mistakes during EC duty, and how can you avoid making these mistakes?

The number one reason most trainees make mistakes early on during EC Duty is they are unsure of what they are supposed to do. How to avoid this: it is the job of the EC Monitor (a detail assignment explained earlier) to ensure that everyone is trained for EC Duty. The tendency of EC Monitors is to quickly explain the process to you because he is in a hurry to train the rest of the Flight. During your training, do not hesitate to ask questions and insist the EC Monitor run a scenario (with you being the person entering) from beginning to end. Then switch roles, with you playing the part of the trainee on EC Duty. By doing this, the EC Monitor will see exactly what you may not understand, and you get practice before the real thing.

Another main cause for mistakes during EC Duty is that MTIs will yell, intimidate, and threaten trainees into letting them enter the dorm without proper access.

How to avoid this: there's no way to avoid the yelling, intimidation, or threats, but you can keep it from causing you to make a mistake. When you're on EC Duty and an MTI is pounding on the door demanding that you let him in, simply do what you were trained to do. Read the EC instructions that are posted on the door, word-for-word and with confidence.

One other common mistake is not allowing access to an MTI who does have proper authority to enter. How to avoid this: be prepared for the MTI who is yelling and threatening, but is not showing proper access identification, to quickly produce the correct identification and demand that you let him in. When this happens do exactly as you were taught and what is said on the posted instructions.

"Do Not" Tips for Night EC Duty

Do not fall asleep. There are two trainees on EC duty for all shifts during the night. Sometimes they get the bright idea to rotate naps throughout their shift. However, there is a high risk that the non-napping trainee will also doze off. Can you guess the result? Right: both trainees are yelled awake and punished by an MTI.

Do not write letters. While it may seem the perfect time to covertly write home, the penalty is severe and the success rate is low.

Do not play practical jokes on sleeping trainees. After a few weeks living in extreme close quarters with the Flight, everyone loosens up around each other. Sometimes people can get too loose and start pulling pranks, and what better time than at night? However, sleep is a precious commodity during basic training and its disturbance won't be taken lightly.

Don't shine your flashlight in the face of those sleeping. If you really need a reason why not to do this, read the answer directly above.

Classroom Instruction

From the beginning to the very end of basic training, you will spend a lot of time in the classroom. It is important to know how to get the most out of the classroom instruction, as you will be expected to either demonstrate it outside of the classroom, or remember it for the written tests. Most of the time, your classroom instructor will not be your MTI. Even though they may not come across as strict, they are still MTIs and expect the same discipline and attention.

One of the hardest things to do in any classroom at basic training is to stay awake. You will be sleep deprived, stressed, and in a new environment, so as soon as you sit down your body automatically wants to rest. Your classroom instructors understand this, and will do what they can to help you stay awake.

Three Effective Ways to Stay Awake During Class

Drink a lot of water (hydrate). Not only will this give your body energy, hydrating will keep you in a constant state of having to use the latrine. This, in turn, will help keep you awake.

Stand Up. Most instructors will tell you to stand at the back of the room if you are having trouble staying awake. Take advantage of the offer before the instructor sees more of your eyelids than your eyeballs. It will save you a lot of trouble and it shows the instructors that you are being proactive.

Take notes and/or highlight. This will help keep you engaged and awake.

If you can stay awake during classes, you have won half the battle to getting the most out of classroom instruction. The other half consists of understanding what is being taught, and understanding what is important. In other words, what will be on the tests? Of course everything that is discussed during class is important, but that fact is that not everything discussed will be on the test. And what is your goal? Your goal is to pass the test.

The best way to understand everything being taught is to ask questions. Even if what you do not understand seems small or stupid, ask your question. "There are no stupid questions, only stupid people," is a popular saying among MTIs. Do not be afraid to ask your instructors questions. Just be sure to go about it the proper way, which will be taught during your first class.

Your instructors are not allowed to tell you what information is on the tests, but it is their job to successfully provide all the information you need to pass the test. In order to do this, your instructors will focus on key material, doing their best to ensure that everyone understands the information. If you pay attention you will easily recognize when your instructors are covering "key" material usually found on the tests.

Here are two key indicators to watch for:

1. The instructor asks specific questions about a topic, or asks multiple trainees to explain the concept in their own words;

2. The instructor repeats a concept or phrase. This is especially important to pay attention to when an instructor rereads a sentence word-for-word out of the book.

When you notice either of these two things, make a note or highlight exactly what the instructor is discussing. Following these simple tips will help you get the most out of classroom instruction.

Weapons Issue

In 2005, the Air Force incorporated the issuing of real weapons at the beginning of basic training. Prior to this, trainees only had one day out of their entire basic training experience to handle a real weapon.

Within your first week at basic training you will be issued an M-16 rifle. You will immediately notice something that sets your weapon apart from ones you may have seen on the news or in the movies: some parts of your weapon are blue. For this reason, you will hear these weapons referred to as "smurf guns." These weapons have been painted blue in order to distinguish them from functional M-16s. While your M-16 is real and has all the parts that allow it to be taken apart and cleaned, it cannot fire. It is important to follow the simple rules laid out by your MTI concerning your M-16. Weapon handling is taken extremely serious by MTIs. Any improper handling of your weapons is a surefire way to get punished or even recycled.

Here are common mistakes trainees make with their weapons:

1. Playing with their weapons in the dorms when they think their MTI is away.

2. Placing the muzzle (the end of the barrel) in the ground.

3. Pointing their weapons at someone inadvertently.

By simply treating your weapon as if it is loaded at all times, you will avoid these common mistakes.

In order to graduate from basic training, you must be able to breakdown (take apart) your weapon within a given time-frame. You will be given plenty of time throughout the first few weeks to practice this. Here are some tips to help you get the most out of your practice time:

1. Once your MTI has shown you how to breakdown and assemble your weapon, go through each step slowly and precisely. Do not rush yourself.

2. Breakdown and assemble the weapon in the same order every time. Even place the individual pieces in the same spot as you breakdown your weapon.

3. When you start going through the steps faster, stop at any step you get stuck on. Rework that step over a few times before moving on.

4. Once you are at the point where you can breakdown and assemble your weapon without stopping, start timing yourself. Either have another trainee time you, or face the large clock located at the end of your bay and time yourself.

Follow these steps. It will help you pass the evaluation.

Being Recycled: A Trainee's Greatest Fear

Being recycled is a trainee's greatest fear during basic. Simply put, being recycled means to be held back in basic training. There are different reasons you can be recycled. Here are the most common:

1. You fail practical application requirements or a written test. You will be given more than one try before being recycled.

2. You fail multiple personal inspections. Throughout basic training there are multiple personal inspections. The first ones are designed to show trainees what is expected. Do not get discouraged if you fail the first one. When you fail an inspection you will be given another chance to pass it. Trainees who fail inspections time after time will be recycled.

3. You get injured. This is the most common reason trainees are recycled. Any injury that prevents you from performing everyday activities will result in you being pulled out of the Flight and sent to a Squadron (the 319th) specifically for trainees with medical conditions that prevent them from training. Any time spent at the 319th does not count toward training. If you spend two weeks at the 319th, when you get out, you must return to whatever week of training you were in before the injury. This means you'll be placed into a different Flight than the one you entered basic training with.

4. You get sick. If you get sick enough that you are unable to perform everyday activities you will be sent to the 319th. However, there is the possibility of recovering in time for you to re-enter your original Flight. This depends on what training you missed and if you are able to make up for it. Example: The dorm chief of my Flight developed a fever toward the end of

basic training. Eventually it got to the point where he was sent to the 319th. After three days his fever dropped just enough for him leave the 319th. He was allowed to return to our Flight by making up the activities he missed. (Don't be surprised if you get a head or chest cold—many trainees catch something during basic training. You will not be recycled for this reason.)

The Truth about Being Recycled

If you talk with Air Force members before you enter basic training, you are sure to hear different horror stories about trainees being recycled for little or no reason. That truth is that the Air Force does not want to recycle trainees. From the Air Force's point of view, recycling a trainee wastes time, resources, and money. For this reason, an MTI must have a good reason and solid documentation for recycling any trainee. You will be given every chance to fix your mistakes (and everyone will make plenty), retake tests, and heal from any injury or sickness before the decision is made to recycle you. The key to not being recycled (besides not getting sick or injured) is to correct any mistakes you make, do your best not to make the same mistakes again, and learn from other trainees' mistakes.

When Will I Get To Call Home?

This is by far the first and most asked question by recruits going into basic training. It is also one of the most asked questions of new recruits by their parents and spouses.

As mentioned earlier, once you arrive your cell phones will be taken and locked away. Therefore, the only means of calling home is when your MTI either gives you your cell phone back for a short period of time or allows you to use the payphones outside your dorms. (Remember, you can only use them when your MTI gives you permission.) The first phone call home will be during the first week. Your MTI will hand out a piece of paper with an address on it. All phone calls are few and far between. For those on payphones, you must use a pre-paid phone card. The Air Force does not pay for your call. So remember to bring a pre-paid phone card and keep it with you at all times.

As soon as your MTI tells your Flight to get ready to go down to the phones, you may not have time to get into your locker to retrieve it. Some trainees won't have a phone card and will be scrambling to borrow someone else's. Make sure you offer yours. It will be the beginning of building camaraderie, which is essential for succeeding in basic training. Also, do not worry that by letting someone use your phone card, you will run out of minutes for yourself. The phone calls you are allowed to make are always short and sweet.

Once your Flight is lined up in front of the row of payphones, your MTI will tell you how much time you have on the phone, and what you are to say. You will be told to read the information on the piece of paper that your MTI handed out. It is your contact information. Your phone time will be between three to five minutes—just long enough to read the information on the paper.

What happens if you get an answering machine? Your MTI will tell you that an answering machine counts for getting a real person. Why? Because you can leave your message on a machine. If you are forced to leave a message, encourage that person to write you a letter. Mail call is often the best time of the day.

What happens if you don't get anyone or a machine? If you do not reach a person or an answering machine/voicemail, you are allowed to either try again or try a new number. For this reason it is a good idea to have multiple numbers ready to call.

> *Tip:* Experiment with various phone cards before you leave for basic training. Some phone cards have long instructions that can't be bypassed, which wastes a lot of time when you only have three minutes on the phone. Your goal is to find a phone card that allows you to dial the number directly and connect with family and friends as quickly as possible.

What happens if the phone is not working? The payphones often are out of order. If you happen to get one of these, let your MTI know and you will be allowed to get into a different line.

When you are on the phone it may be hard to concentrate because everyone waiting in line will be telling those on the phone that their time is up. If you go over your time (remember, you will be timed) then your MTI will be yelling at you to get off the phone. The best thing to do once someone picks up the other line is to tell them that you only have a couple of minutes and to get a piece of paper and pencil. While they are looking, you can tell them how you are doing. When they are ready to write, speak slowly and clearly. You want to make sure they get your contact information correct.

After the first phone call, it is entirely up to your MTI how many more you get. Phone calls are a way of rewarding the Flight. So, the better the Flight does, as a whole, the more chances you have of making additional phone calls.

Chapter 15

Study Guide

Memory Work

Memory work is a large part of basic training. When you arrive, you will receive a piece of paper that contains names of people, rank structure, pay grade, and other facts. This piece of paper is your memory work. Whenever you are waiting (which you will do a lot), you will be told to get out your memory work.

An MTI can ask you questions from your memory work at anytime during basic training. Whether you answer correctly or not will determine a positive or negative outcome (an incorrect answer will result in a negative consequence). Therefore, it is vital that you memorize the information on the piece of paper as soon as possible. Much of it can be memorized before you arrive at basic training. The rest of the information changes with time, and even depends on what squadron you are in. The following is the memory work that you can and should learn ahead of time.

Rank Structure, Pay Grade, and Insignia

Understand the difference between rank and pay grade. Think of rank as the title, such as Staff Sergeant or Major. Remember that pay grade is a number. E-1, for example, refers to Airman Basic. Notice that the enlisted personnel pay grades all start with an "E" for "enlisted." Officer pay grades start with an "O" which of course stands for "officer."

No Insignia

Rank: Airman Basic
Abbreviation: AB
Pay Grade: E-1
Insignia: No Insignia.

Rank: Airman
Abbreviation: AM
Pay Grade: E-2
Insignia: Chevron of one stripe.

Rank: Airman First Class
Abbreviation: A1C
Pay Grade: E-3
Insignia: Chevron of two stripes.

Rank: Senior Airman
Abbreviation: SrA
Pay Grade: E-4
Insignia: Chevron of three stripes.

Rank: Staff Sergeant
Abbreviation: SSgt
Pay Grade: E-5
Insignia: Chevron of four stripes.

Rank: Technical Sergeant
Abbreviation: TSgt
Pay Grade: E-6
Insignia: Chevron of five stripes.

Rank: Master Sergeant
Abbreviation: MSgt
Pay Grade: E-7
Insignia: Chevron of six stripes, with one inverted.

Rank: Senior Master Sergeant
Abbreviation: SMSgt
Pay Grade: E-8
Insignia: Chevron of seven stripes, with two inverted.

Rank: Chief Master Sergeant
Abbreviation: CMSgt
Pay Grade: E-9
Insignia: Chevron of Eight stripes, with three inverted.

Position: First Sergeant
Abbreviation: 1st Sgt
Pay Grade: E-7: E9
Insignia: Chevron of six, seven or eight stripes, and a diamond.

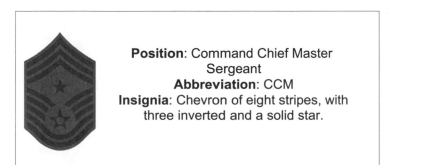

Position: Command Chief Master Sergeant
Abbreviation: CCM
Insignia: Chevron of eight stripes, with three inverted and a solid star.

Position: Chief Master Sergeant of the Air Force
Abbreviation: CMSAF
Insignia: Chevron of eight stripes, with three inverted, with a wreath around the star in the lower field. The Great Seal of the United States of America with a star flanked on either side in the upper field.

The information provided below is what you will should absolutely memorize before you leave for basic training. An MTI will ask you a number of questions based upon this information. Here are the types of questions you will be asked, followed by the correct answers.

Note: Begin with the reporting statement first if you have not already given it.

MTI : What is the pay grade of a Staff Sergeant?
Trainee: The pay grade of a Staff Sergeant is E-5.

MTI: Describe the rank insignia of a Master Sergeant.
Trainee: The rank insignia of Master Sergeant is, a chevron of six stripes with one inverted.

MTI: What is the rank of an E-6?
Trainee: The rank of an E-6 is Technical Sergeant.

Notice that before answering any of these questions that you repeat the question. This is important to remember.

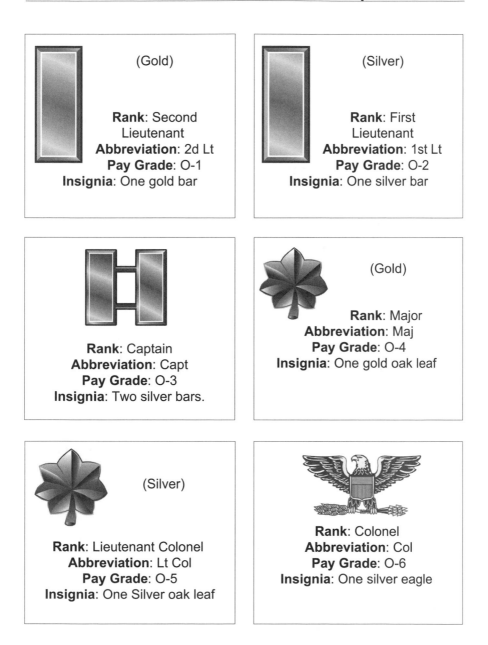

(Gold)

Rank: Second Lieutenant
Abbreviation: 2d Lt
Pay Grade: O-1
Insignia: One gold bar

(Silver)

Rank: First Lieutenant
Abbreviation: 1st Lt
Pay Grade: O-2
Insignia: One silver bar

Rank: Captain
Abbreviation: Capt
Pay Grade: O-3
Insignia: Two silver bars.

(Gold)

Rank: Major
Abbreviation: Maj
Pay Grade: O-4
Insignia: One gold oak leaf

(Silver)

Rank: Lieutenant Colonel
Abbreviation: Lt Col
Pay Grade: O-5
Insignia: One Silver oak leaf

Rank: Colonel
Abbreviation: Col
Pay Grade: O-6
Insignia: One silver eagle

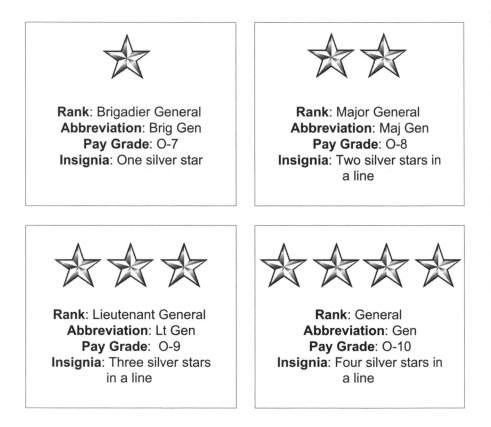

Rank: Brigadier General
Abbreviation: Brig Gen
Pay Grade: O-7
Insignia: One silver star

Rank: Major General
Abbreviation: Maj Gen
Pay Grade: O-8
Insignia: Two silver stars in a line

Rank: Lieutenant General
Abbreviation: Lt Gen
Pay Grade: O-9
Insignia: Three silver stars in a line

Rank: General
Abbreviation: Gen
Pay Grade: O-10
Insignia: Four silver stars in a line

Here is a simple trick to memorize the order of rank for the generals. Remember the following sentence:

By   My   Little   General

This stands for: Brigadier, Major, and Lieutenant General (with the latter rank being the highest).

Chain of Command

You MUST memorize the chain of command. This starts with the President of the United States as the Commander in Chief and goes all the way down to your dorm chief. As you can see from the chart on the next page, many of the individuals in your chain of command are part of the training squadron to which you will be assigned. Because you will not know your training squadron until you arrive, there is no way to memorize those individuals ahead of time.

However, you are able to memorize the individuals that hold the positions from the President of the United States down to the commander of the 737th Training Group. Current Air Force Command information can be found on the Lackland Air Force Base website under "library + biographies."

By memorizing what you can now about the chain of command, you will be saving yourself a lot of work and stress during basic training. Use the provided sheet to fill in and memorize the positions.

CHAIN OF COMMAND	
President of the United States	
Secretary of Defense	
Secretary of the Air Force	
Chief of Staff of the Air Force	
Chief Master Sergeant of the Air Force	
Commander, Air Education & Training Command	
Commander, 2nd Air Force	
Commander, 37th Training Wing (37th TRW)	
Vice Commander, 37th TRW	
Command Chief Master Sergeant, 37th TRW	
Commander, 737th Training Group (TRG)	

Deputy Commander, 737th TRG	Wait until basic training
Superintendent, 737 TRG	Wait until basic training
Squadron Commander	Wait until basic training
Operations Officer	Wait until basic training
Training Superintendent	Wait until basic training
First Sergeant	Wait until basic training
Section Supervisor	Wait until basic training
Instructor Team	Wait until basic training
Dorm Chief	Wait until basic training
Weapon Serial Number	Wait until basic training

Air Force Core Values

1. Integrity First
2. Service Before Self
3. Excellence in All We Do

Airman's Creed

During basic, you'll get lots of practice saying the Airman's Creed. Before starting any classroom session, you'll say it:

I am an American Airman.
I am a Warrior.
I have answered my Nation's call.

I am an American Airman.
My mission is to Fly, Fight, and Win.
I am faithful to a Proud Heritage,

A Tradition of Honor,
And a Legacy of Valor.

I am an American Airman.
Guardian of Freedom and Justice,
My Nation's Sword and Shield,
Its Sentry and Avenger.
I defend my Country with my Life.

I am an American Airman.
Wingman, Leader, Warrior.
I will never leave an Airman behind,
I will never falter,
And I will not fail.

Military Time (24-Hour Clock)

Civilians use the 12-hour clock. In the military and during basic training, you will use the 24-hour clock. While you will not normally be tested on this information, it is important to understand military time because it will be used exclusively throughout your training. To convert civilian time to military time, just add 12 hours to every hour past noon. For example: 4:00 p.m. in military time is 1600 hours (12 + 4=16). The table below shows you how to convert these times.

(Note: When you write the date in military time, it should be day/month/year. For example April 2, 2004, is 02Apr04.)

HOW TO READ MILITARY TIME		
CIVILIAN TIME	**MILITARY TIME**	**PRONUNCIATION**
12:01 a.m.	0001	zero zero zero one
1:00 a.m.	0100	zero one hundred hours

CIVILIAN TIME	MILITARY TIME	PRONUNCIATION
2:00 a.m.	0200	zero two hundred hours
3:00 a.m.	0300	zero three hundred hours
4:00 a.m.	0400	zero four hundred hours
5:00 a.m.	0500	zero five hundred hours
6:00 a.m.	0600	zero six hundred hours
7:00 a.m.	0700	zero seven hundred hours
8:00 a.m.	0800	zero eight hundred hours
9:00 a.m.	0900	zero nine hundred hours
10:00 a.m.	1000	ten hundred hours
11:00 a.m.	1100	eleven hundred hours
12:00 noon	1200	twelve hundred hours
1:00 p.m.	1300	thirteen hundred hours
2:00 p.m.	1400	fourteen hundred hours
3:00 p.m.	1500	fifteen hundred hours
4:00 p.m.	1600	sixteen hundred hours
5:00 p.m.	1700	seventeen hundred hours
6:00 p.m.	1800	eighteen hundred hours
7:00 p.m.	1900	nineteen hundred hours
8:00 p.m.	2000	twenty hundred hours
9:00 p.m.	2100	twenty-one hundred hours

CIVILIAN TIME	MILITARY TIME	PRONUNCIATION
10:00 p.m.	2200	twenty-two hundred hours
11:00 p.m.	2300	twenty-three hundred hours
12:00 midnight	2400	twenty-four hundred hours
8:36 a.m.	0836	zero eight thirty-six
11:52 a.m.	1152	eleven fifty-two
12:06 p.m.	1206	twelve zero six
3:11 p.m.	1511	fifteen eleven
10:41p.m.	2241	twenty-two forty-one

Hydration Schedule

Not only are you required to follow the hydration schedule, you are required to memorize it: *I must drink ½ to ¾ of a canteen every hour. I will not exceed 12 canteens in one day.*

10 Tips For Passing Written Tests

You take two written tests during basic training. You must pass both each with 70% or higher to continue with training. Here are a few tips to help you pass, and in turn complete basic training on time.

1. Take time to study alone. Before going over the test material with other trainees, study by yourself. This ensures that you cover any and all the material you may be unclear about.

2. Study in a group. When studying in a group it is best to quiz each other on information. By taking turns quizzing one another, everyone benefits from the time spent together.

3. Do not "cram" the night before. If you study periodically throughout training, you will avoid trying to learn it all in one night.

4. Relax. Once you get to the classroom to take the test, you will be handed a pencil and the test. While everyone is getting situated take this time to get your mind focused on the test. Remember to breathe.

5. Read every question carefully. Take the time to understand each and every question. Many trainees answer questions incorrectly simply because they rushed through the question. Take your time.

6. Answer every question. Any questions left unanswered are counted as wrong answers. Therefore it is important to answer every question whether or not you know the answer.

7. Use the process of elimination. Both tests you will take are multiple choice, in bubble format. Fill in the correct bubble for each question. You will have multiple answers to choose from. In situations where you do not know the answer, you can usually make an "educated guess," by eliminating the answers that you know are incorrect. This way, instead of guessing from four possible answers, you can be guessing from two possible answers.

8. Answer the question in your head before looking at the available answers. Always read the question, understand the question, and answer the question in your head before even looking at the possible answers listed. If your answer is one of the answers available, then that is most likely the correct answer.

9. Don't change your answer. More often than not, your first answer is the correct answer.

10. Review all your answers. Once you have completed the test, go back to the beginning and review to make sure that you answered every question, and that you filled in the correct bubble. A common mistake made on multiple choice bubble tests is, knowing the correct answer, but accidentally filling in the wrong bubble.

Chapter 16

Weeks 2 – 4:
The Pressure Rises

As you progress further along in basic training, more is expected of you. By your second week, MTIs will be pulling you aside to drill you on your memory retention. By your fourth week, making simple mistakes, such as improper facing movements, offering an incorrect reporting statement, or forgetting to put your cover on or take it off, will have bigger consequences. By this time, you will be expected to know better. So the best thing is to learn as much as you can now, before basic training.

341

The official title for a 341 is "Excellence/Discrepancy Report." The 341 is a small piece of paper that contains your name, organizations, flight number, roster number, and grade. 341s are used by MTIs to document trainee's actions of excellence—or actions that required discipline. The truth is that 99% of the time they are "pulled" (taken and written on) for a disciplinary action. Don't be too disappointed or surprised to have a 341 pulled; most trainees will experience this at least once, and likely more than that.

EXCELLENCE/DISCREPANCY REPORT	
LAST NAME – FIRST NAME –MIDDLE INITIAL	GRADE
Excellence/Exhibited Discrepancy (be specific)	
This is where the MTI would write exactly why you are in trouble, or how you did a good job (but the latter is not likely).	
TIME:_____ DATE:_____ PLACE:_____	
PRINTED NAME OF REPORTING INDIVIDUAL	SIGNATURE OF REPORTING INDIVIDUAL

Consequences

The consequences for having a 341 pulled vary depending on the circumstances, and how many you have already had pulled that Week of Training (WOT). When an MTI other than your own pulls your 341, that MTI will state the reason disciplinary action is needed, or why you should be rewarded. That 341 will be turned in to your MTI, who will decide on the appropriate action to be taken. If you have a 341 pulled and you never sign it, it will not go on record as having been pulled.

Example: During an inspection, my MTI pulled every trainee's 341 for not shaving well enough. However, only the trainees that had a recurring problem with shaving had their 341 recorded.

Giving a 341

One of the many phrases that will ring in your ears during basic training is "Give me a 341!" Hopefully, you hear this being said more often to other trainees than to you. However, odds are that you will have at least one 341 pulled during your time at basic training. The worst thing you can do when told to give a 341 is not to have one with you. You will be told to carry two 341s at all times. I suggest carrying three just to be safe. They often get lost, go through the wash, or simply become too dirty for an MTI to touch.

The second worst thing you can do is to not have your 341 filled out correctly. Always make sure you fill in <u>every</u> box on your 341s.

The third worst thing you can to do is to dig through your pockets, franticly looking for one. MTIs thrive on this. What better time to get in your face then when you are taking too long to do something so simple. Don't let this happen to you. Prepare one 341 so that it is always ready and available. Fold it in half lengthwise two times. At one end, fold it down about half an inch. Use the folded end as a hook, and hook it to the top of your pants cargo pocket. Your pocket flap will cover the end that is hooked. Now, if you are told to give a 341, you can quickly and effortlessly retrieve it, unfold it, and hand it over. This will actually surprise the MTI, though they won't show it.

Wall Locker Inspections

The wall locker inspections are one of the most stressful events in basic training. You spend hours making sure everything is just right, and an MTI literally tears it all apart in a matter of seconds, and tells you that you didn't do anything right. Expect this and you won't be surprised or disappointed. Remember, nothing is personal. So you do it again, and again you find your uniforms scattered across your bunk as a sign that you did it wrong. Here are a few tips you need to know to pass your wall locker inspections.

As part of the Air Force BMT restructuring, the wall locker set-up has also been revised. It has been simplified so it does not take as long to do, which leaves more time for additional training. However, this does not mean that standards have been dropped. Believe it or not, your wall locker is a representation of your dedication and "attention to detail." Many trainees never understand why so much stress is put on having their wall lockers perfect at all times. The Air Force is not about to entrust you with repairing a jet, working with classified documents, or protecting an air base if you can't pay attention and make sure your socks are facing in the right direction. (The attention to detail with your wall locker only applies during basic training).

ABUs

One of the most common demerits (negative points) given for ABUs is for strings. With so many seams and pockets, your ABUs will seem to have an endless supply of loose strings. It is your job to cut off every one of them. A simple way to ensure that you get all of them is to use the following method:

> *TIP: With your ABU top (blouse) on a hanger, start from the top and cut the strings working your way down. As you go down work from your left to your right (like reading). Follow this pattern to avoid missing any areas. Why this way? Because when you cut the strings off they fall down, and many of them will cling to the ABU. As you go down you will naturally come across these loose stings and brush them off. Once you have done the front, turn it over and do the back!*
>
> *ABU pants: lay them flat on a bed and use the same pattern. You will also want to double-check them for any loose strings that may have been on the bed and stuck to the back of the pants.*

T-Shirts

ABU t-shirts are now rolled into a tube shape instead of folded into perfect squares. The biggest difficulty in rolling t-shirts is not having any wrinkle showing. Many trainees will spend too much time trying to get wrinkles out of a rolled t-shirt. This does not work. The key is to make sure the t-shirt is wrinkle free from the very beginning. Here is a tip on how to do this:

> *TIP: Place your t-shirt flat on your bed. Fill your canteen with very hot water from the latrine. Then, use your canteen as an iron, and iron any wrinkles out of the shirt as best you can. After that, keep the shirt flat and fix any wrinkles as you go along.*

Another problem is keeping your rolled t-shirts rolled tightly once you've finished. Take two of blousing straps (elastic straps for keeping your pant legs tucked up) and wrap them once around your rolled shirt. Keep them on until you have finished with your wall locker; take them off right before putting your shirts in your locker.

Socks

Rolling socks can be a two-person operation. One person holds one end whiles the other rolls. This helps ensure the socks are rolled tightly like they're supposed to be. While this builds teamwork and makes everyone work as a Flight, there will be times when you just need to get your socks done and no one will be available to assist. The key is to find something to hold your socks on one end so that you can pull them tight and roll them up.

TIP: Your wall locker door works great for this. Open the door, place the open ends of the socks on the top ridge of the door, and close your socks in the door. Your wall locker door will now do the holding, while you do the rolling.

Security Drawer

Your wall locker consists of two drawers. The top one is your security drawer. What makes it a security drawer is that it is the only part of your wall locker that can be locked. Inside this drawer are all your personal records, miscellaneous items, and toiletries. You must keep your security drawer clean and in order, just like the rest of your wall locker. If you leave their security drawer unorganized you will get a demerit. Here are two other main causes why trainees get demerits: (1) dirty razor; (2) dirty towel that lines the bottom of the drawer. The simplest way to never have a dirty razor, is to never use it.

TIP: Keep an unused disposable razor in the display area of your security drawer, and keep the ones you use in the pack. If you use an electric razor, you can still keep a disposable razor on display.

The bottom of your security drawer is lined with a white towel. Ironically, the main way it gets dirty is shampoo. After using your shampoo, the bottle has a tendency to either drip or leak. Either way it leaves a stain the color of the shampoo on your white towel. The easiest way to avoid having colored spots on your towel—which equals demerits—is to bring or buy white shampoo. This way, even if it leaks it won't leave a stain that will be noticed.

Second Clothing Issue

Your second clothing issue is when you receive your dress uniform "blues." This is nothing like your first clothing issue. This will probably be the first, and maybe the last time in the Air Force that you have a set of clothes measured and sewn to fit you specifically.

Even though the people fitting, measuring, and sewing your uniform are civilians, you must maintain your military bearing and behavior. The civilians you come in contact with during basic training can be more difficult than military personnel! Worse, some will treat you with "MTI methods" even though they do not have MTI training to know when, why, or how these methods are used.

For the most part, all you need to do during this time is be where you're supposed to be and stand still while you're getting fitted. The two clothing items you do have more of a say about are your shoes and your flight cap. Your shoes are the most important of the two. Make sure you dress shoes fit well. They're not very comfortable to begin with, so you don't want them too large or too small. Even if you don't plan on wearing them after basic training, you will be in them for long periods of time during basic training. Regarding your flight cap, make sure that it isn't too big. If it feels a bit too small, that means it fits.

You will also have wall locker inspections once you get your dress uniforms. Be sure to check your shirt and pants pockets when preparing your dress uniform for inspection. Little pieces of paper are in the pockets of every clothing item (the manufacture inspection tags), and they are worth a demerit if an MTI finds one during inspection. Otherwise, follow the same routine as with your ABUs.

Obstacle Course

For many trainees this is one of the highlights of basic training. Think of the obstacle course as a gigantic playground—a jungle gym with balance beams, a rope swing, monkey bars, tubes to crawl through, walls to climb, and water to make it that much more fun!

Is the obstacle course hard? Yes—because of its length. It seems to go on and on, and as it does, the obstacles get harder and harder and involve water. (The goal is to stay out of the water.) Here are a few tips on how to get through the obstacle course successfully, if not dry.

1. Go through with a partner and keep each other motivated.

2. Pace yourself. Remember some of the final obstacles are the hardest. Save some energy for these.

3. Don't give up. You are required to complete the course to graduate, so make it through each obstacle one way or another.

4. Don't panic. Some trainees go overboard during the obstacle course, which can result in injury, which can result in . . . recycling.

5. Listen to the instructors. All the way through the obstacle course, there are instructors posted to instruct you when and where to go.

6. Catch the rope! One of the last obstacles is the rope swing above water. The rope will be swinging and the goal is to jump, catch the rope, and swing to the far side. If the rope is not swinging right, the instructor will tell you not to jump. Otherwise, catch the rope!

Church Services

During basic training, the Air Force provides a number of different church services for trainees. All church services are held on Sundays regardless of religion or denomination. You have a choice of what service you want to attend, or if you want to attend at all. If you do not attend a church service you will remain in the dorms and your MTI will find something for you to do. This is not punishment; your MTI just isn't going to let you hang around and do nothing.

Many trainees who do not regularly attend a church end up going to church during basic training. Here are some reasons why:

1. There are not MTIs at or around church services.

2. You are encouraged to smile at church (unlike elsewhere).

3. The chaplains understand what you are going through and are encouraging.

On your first Sunday morning you will have a chapel guide who is a trainee further along in training than you. This trainee will show you where to go. After that you will go on your own with other trainees in your Flight. Be sure to remember your military bearing at all times, including on your way to church service.

While in service, the most important thing to remember is not to fall asleep. You can still have 341s pulled during church! There are Sunday school classes available after church. Again, you can choose from different religions and denominations. The teachers for these classes are civilians from different churches and organizations.

LIST OF SERVICES			
Catholic	Jewish	Eastern Orthodox	Pentecostal
Seventh-Day Adventist	Church of Christ	Christian Science	Latter-day Saints
Liturgical Protestant (Episcopal, Lutheran, Congregational)	Protestant (Baptist, Methodist, Presbyterian)	Buddhist	Hindu
Baha'i	Eckankar	Wicca	Muslim

Making Appointments

Different circumstances will come up that will require you to miss some training for an appointment. It could be for financial matters, to see a doctor, exchange dress shoes for ones that fit, and so on.

Your MTI will schedule your appointments so you do not miss any critical training. Because of this, you may not get to an appointment for several days (unless it is for medical reasons). Let your MTI know exactly what the appointment is for. Never tell your MTI you need to go to an appointment. Always request to go to an appointment.

Medical

Because it's common for trainees to get sick during basic training, there are many requests for medical attention. If you feel sick, request to get a cold pack (a bag of different medications, i.e., aspirin, cough drops, etc). However, if it is more than a cold, then explain exactly to your MTI what you are suffering from (fever, flu, etc.). Let your MTI know of any medical issues (other than a cold) during the weekdays, since this is when the different medical services are open.

Other Appointments

The key to requesting appointments is to know when to approach your MTI. Don't be the trainee who does it when the Flight is getting ready to go somewhere, or when the MTI just walked in the dorm. Wait until your MTI is in the flight office. This is the best time to request an appointment. By doing it then, your MTI will be able to look at the week's schedule and write down your request.

Chapter 17

The Gas Chamber

Every trainee who goes through basic training will go through nuclear, biological, and chemical (NBC) training. That means you will be subjected to training in "the gas chamber."

Many recruits worry about this training so much that the stress is worse than the actual experience! Why the need to go through the gas chamber in the first place? To provide you with confidence that your NBC equipment (e.g., protective mask) will work when you really need it. Confidence in your equipment will mean a great deal if you need to use it in a real life situation.

What is the Gas Chamber?

The gas chamber is a room with a controlled concentration of CS gas (orto-chlorobenzylidene-malononitrile), more commonly known as "tear gas"). Tear gas is the active ingredient in Mace™ and is used for self-defense and riot control by law enforcement. Tear gas irritates mucous membranes in the eyes, nose, mouth, and lungs. The irritating effect causes tearing, sneezing, coughing, and discomfort.

The Process

Usually, during your fourth week of basic training, you will experience the gas chamber. You have access to your daily schedule, so you will know in advance when you are slated for this training. If you are scheduled to go to the gas chamber in the afternoon, I suggest eating a light lunch. Sucking in a lungful of tear gas on a full stomach rarely sits well on a full stomach.

Before entering the gas chamber you will go through extensive training on how to fit your protective mask and chemical gear. You will take this training with additional Flights, and the instructors want to make sure everyone understands what to do. Therefore, they will take a lot of time to make sure everyone understands what to do—and what not to do. It is vital that you follow their instructions to the letter. Making a mistake during this training could get you recycled.

TIP: Never be farther than arms-reach away from your gas mask during this training. If you are caught without it, you will automatically fail and be pulled out of training.

When everyone is properly suited up, you will stand in one of many lines formed outside the gas chambers. Then you will wait, as you watch trainee after trainee go into the gas chamber. You will enter the gas chamber with about 20 other trainees. The room will be very foggy. The fog you see is CS gas. You may smell it slightly through your mask. You will file into the gas chamber and stand along the wall facing the center. In the center of the room you will see a brick box. The CS gas is coming from that box. The instructor will have you do jumping jacks and other activities to make sure you are breathing deeply and not trying to hold your breath. (If you are wearing your gear properly you will not have any trouble.)

Then, one by one, the instructor will have you and the other trainees remove your gas masks. To make sure you are not holding your breath, you will have to say your reporting statement to the instructor with your gas mask off. Once the instructor is satisfied, he will open the door and you will be allowed to exit the gas chamber. It is important not to move toward the door until you are told to leave. If you do, you will not be allowed to leave until the next trainee has gone. And you will not have your mask on during that time!

The Treatment

As you exit the gas chamber, your eyes will be filling with water and your lungs and face will be filling with mucous. The best treatment is clean air. Open your eyes as soon as you exit the gas chamber. This will seem hard to do because your eyes are burning, but keeping your eyes open in fresh air will dissipate the burning and discomfort very quickly.

> *TIP: Even though you will want to, do not touch your face. Touching and rubbing your face is the worst thing you can do at this point in the training. This is why MTIs will be yelling at you as you exit, "Hold your arms out!" By not touching your face and taking deep breaths, the CS will leave your system quickly. In less then a minute you will be nearly back to normal.*

Directly after the gas chamber training you will go on a run with your Flight. This will help cleanse your body of the tear gas and trust me, the run will feel great. Afterwards, you will go shower and continue with training—with the dreaded gas chamber behind you forever.

Chapter 18

Week 5: More Stress, Less Time . . . No Problem

The fifth week consists of a lot of classroom time to prepare you for the B.E.A.S.T, which occurs during week six. You will be required to take the information from these classes and apply it directly to the next week of training. (Be sure to use the classroom tips from Chapter 14.) In addition to classroom instruction, week five includes two hands-on training events: the M16 live fire, and pugil stick fighting.

M16 Weapons Live Fire

By this time you will have learned the basics of weapons safety and weapons cleaning by using your smurf gun. Now you will put these skills to practical use. Leaving your smurf guns behind, your Flight will take a bus ride to the firing range. The range is operated by Combat Arms Training and Maintenance (CATM) instructors, all of whom are Security Forces members. They are not MTIs, but still demand your full attention and respect.

The first part of your day will be spent in a classroom. However, this phase of the instruction is very hands-on. You will be reviewing safety procedures and learning how to operate and shoot the M16 rifle. While it is important to pay attention to your instructors throughout all of basic training, failing to do so during weapons training could result in a fatal accident. Here are three common mistakes trainees make (but since you have read this book, you will avoid them):

1. Don't touch the weapon until you are told to.

2. When handling the weapon, do not point it at anyone, especially an instructor.

3. Do not pull the trigger, except when told to do so (even when the weapon isn't loaded).

The Firing Range

After a few hours it will feel as if you the class will never end, mostly because the instructors will have you constantly repeat the safety and operating procedures before moving to the firing range.

The firing training consists of three parts. First, you will shoot to make sure your M16 is correctly sighted; this is called "zeroing in." Once the bullets are hitting where you are aiming, you will go through a series of shooting routines. You will practice shooting standing up, lying down, kneeling, etc. This is the time to get comfortable with your weapon. Get used to the feel of the rifle in your hands, the sound of it when it shoots, and the feel and sound of it when it jams (i.e., doesn't shoot when you pull the trigger).

After this, you will begin the qualifications portion of the training. This consists of the same shooting routines you just practiced—only now you are being timed. You will shoot 40 rounds (bullets) during qualifications. In order to qualify you must hit the target with 20 of the rounds. If you want to qualify as "expert" (and get the Small Arms Expert Ribbon), you must hit the target with 35 of the 40 rounds.

How to Qualify as Expert

The instructors often tell you that the trainees who shoot the best are the ones with no previous experience. Why is this? Because these trainees are coming to the shooting range with no bad habits, and the instructors are able to teach them the correct way to shoot. With the influence of video games, paint ball, and air soft, instructors find many trainees have formed habits that only hinder their ability to shoot accurately. During your practice shooting, erase from your mind what you know, or think you know, about shooting and do it the way the instructors teach you. As you get comfortable with the weapon, you will find that the instructor's "correct" way of shooting works. If you have shooting experience and learned the correct way to begin with, the instructors will be only be emphasizing what you already know.

If you follow these few shooting guidelines with every shot you take, you can shoot "expert" on the M16 rifle.

Shoot your own target. As impossible as it seems, a common mistake (and one that keeps trainees from qualifying) is shooting their neighbor's target instead of their own.

Relax. Even for people who have a lot of experience shooting weapons, qualifying can be stressful. Relax by breathing regularly. Many trainees hold their breath, which in turn results in short and jerky breaths, which in turn causes their weapon to jerk.

Shoot on your exhale. After you have set your sight on the target, take a complete breath in. At the end of your exhale (the natural respiratory pause), hold your breath and squeeze the trigger.

Squeeze, don't jerk. When pulling the trigger, pull smoothly and in one motion. By pulling the trigger quickly, you are actually moving your weapon enough to miss your target. (During this training, accuracy counts more than speed.).

Imagine that each shot is a dry fire (no bullet in the weapon). Every time you pull the trigger, pretend that there is no bullet in the weapon and that your goal is to keep your sight on the target the entire time you are pulling and releasing the trigger.

Use your previous shot as a gauge. When one of your shots hits the black target, you will see a white dot it leaves behind. Use this as a marker to gauge where you need to aim next. If one of your shots is in or near the middle of the target, aim for that spot.

Pugil Stick Fighting

For years the Army and Marines have been using pugil stick fighting in basic training. The Air Force has recently incorporated it into basic training as part of the new "Warrior Airman" concept. Being a "Warrior Airman" means that as an Airman you are a warrior first, and a fuels specialist, jet engine mechanic (or whatever your job is) second. When you get to your duty station you will do the specific job you are trained to do. However, the Air Force wants all Airmen to be capable of defending the base. Therefore, pugil stick fighting is now a part of basic training (and it has quickly become one of the favorite events among trainees).

Pugil stick fighting simulates using your M16 in hand-to-hand combat. First, you will be taught different striking techniques with your M16, and then you will have the chance to put them to practice using pugil sticks.

A pugil stick resembles a large Q-tip. The two padded ends are used to hit your opponent (another member of your Flight). During pugil stick fighting trainees are supposed to utilize the rifle fighting techniques, but most trainees resort to random swings and sloppy blows. Here are eight tips on how to put your opponent down while you remain on your feet.

1. Use the techniques you are taught (they actually work).

2. Keep your stick close to your body. When your arms are extended out in front of you, any blows you make will be virtually ineffective.

3. Hold your pugil stick at an angle and up high to protect your upper body and head.

4. Stand facing your opponent at an angle. Place your weak foot forward and bend at the knees.

5. Don't stand directly in front of your opponent. Position yourself slightly to the right or left of your opponent (depending on if your left or right-handed. If your right-handed stand to the right). This makes it harder for your opponent to hit you.

6. Don't stand in one place. Move from side to side in order to stay off center from your opponent.

7. When you take a hit, don't stop or freeze. The ability to get hit and keep fighting is just as important as being able to hit your opponent.

8. When you hit your opponent successfully, don't stop. If possible, continue to strike him until you are told to stop.

And of course, have fun!

Getting Paid

During the fourth or fifth week of training you will receive your first military paycheck. The money will go directly into your direct deposit account, and your MTI will post a sheet that will show how much money was deposited. The initial response from trainees when they see this sheet is to think they did not get paid the correct amount.

Keep in mind that this first paycheck is your base pay (it does not include any food or housing allowances) less the amount taken out for your uniforms and other gear issued to you during basic training. I would recommend that before entering basic training you make sure you have enough money set aside to last at least two months.

Don't be surprised to find that some trainees are getting paid more or less than you. There are many reasons for trainees to get paid different amounts. Some of these reasons have to do with rank, marriage status, and dependent status.

What if my Pay is Wrong?

Sometimes a trainee does not get paid the correct amount. In fact, you will be told that if your pay is less than $100.00 to let you MTI know. If your pay is incorrect, ask your MTI to make an appointment for you with the financial office. Your MTI must let you go to this appointment to fix your finances.

When you meet with the personnel at the finance office, explain why you are there. They will ask you how you know the amount is wrong because many trainees will be coming in to complain about the same thing—and their pay is actually correct!

Don't let this discourage you from going in and seeing them. You are responsible for keeping track of you personal finances and that is exactly what you are doing when checking in with the finance office.

Air National Guard Pay

If you are in the Air National Guard and you do not believe your pay is correct, do not go the financial office. You will need to see the Guard Liaison. They will contact your base and be able to see if there is a discrepancy.

Chapter 19

Dress Faster Than Superman

With all the activities the MTIs schedule during your day, it is little wonder why they make you change clothes so fast. Many trainees are late to formation because they can't seem to get dressed in five minutes (30 seconds, MTI time). Believe it or not, you can prepare a host of little things that the vast majority of your fellow trainees will never think of doing. By thinking and planning ahead, you can make your life easier by giving more reasons for the MTI to pick on someone other than you, and get dressed much faster and never be late to formation.

Physical Readiness Training (PRT) Mornings

You will wake up each morning at 4:30 a.m. and everyone must be out of the dorm and on the pad by 4:45 a.m. This gives you (and everyone else) fifteen minutes to get dressed, brush your teeth, shave, make your bunk, and get downstairs. If you have PRT in the morning (which is normal except during the cold months), getting dressed won't take long. However, the less time you spend getting dressed the better.

The night before, find out what your first activity of the day will be. If it is PRT, get out your PRT uniform (shorts, t-shirt, and socks) and put it on. This way you won't have to spend time getting into your locker. Now, when you get up all you have to do is put your shoes on and you're dressed.

Non-PRT Morning

There will be days that PRT is not the first thing you do. This means that within those frantic first fifteen minutes of the day you will have to dress in your ABUs—and you can't wear these to bed. What to do? Simple. The night before, put on your ABU t-shirt and green socks. Once again, this eliminates spending time getting into your locker, and eliminates the time it takes to put your socks and shirt on.

Preparing Your Uniform

Whether you are dressing in your ABUs in the morning or the middle of the day, make sure your uniform is prepared properly. Hanging on the outside of your locker is the uniform you will be wearing that day. In your locker drawer are your socks and t-shirts. Make sure everything is hung, rolled, and placed to your MTI's specifications. Not only is this the only way you will pass inspections, but these specifications are designed to help you get dressed faster than the next guy.

Do a Double Check

Before you go to bed at night, it is always a good idea to make a habit of checking the buttons on your uniform to make sure the correct ones are buttoned. Once your uniform is hung on the outside of your locker, smooth over the fabric with your hands to make sure all the wrinkles are flattened out as much as possible. MTIs do not like uniforms with wrinkles.

The Mental Race to Your Wall Locker

Once your MTI releases you from formation and gives you three minutes to change, it is time to run to your wall locker and find your prepared clothes. But before you do that, let's discuss the run to your wall locker.

While making your way to the locker, you should be mentally thinking of everything you need to bring to formation and where it is in your wall locker. By mentally preparing yourself, you will already know what you need to grab by the time that wall locker flies opens.

Now it is time to get dressed. Before you even touch the clothes you are going to wear, get all the clothes you are wearing off and put away. They will usually go into your laundry bag, which hangs at the end of your bunk. Think about it. Instead of taking things off, putting them down, finding them in the midst of other peoples clothes, and picking them back up again to put them away, you save time by only handling each article of clothing once. The last thing you want to be doing at the end of those three minutes is scrambling to find your PRT shorts you just took off. It is almost as bad as never finding them and explaining to your MTI that you lost your clothes.

After taking off your clothes, the first thing that should go on your body is your t-shirt. Putting on your t-shirt first means you don't have to tuck it into your pants later. After the t-shirt come the socks, followed by the pants. Since you left the top two buttons undone, the pants will fit easily around the t-shirt that needs to be tucked in. So while everyone else is trying to tuck their t-shirts into their pants, you will be lacing up your boots.

By now you should have everything on but your ABU blouse. I recommend that you put this on last because it has your name on it. You will usually be changing with many other trainees in tight quarters. With all those articles of clothing lying around, it is not uncommon for clothes to get mixed between trainees. Once your ABU blouse is on, just grab your hat (cover) and any miscellaneous gear your MTI requires you bring—and you are ready to go!

Chapter 20

Week 6: Conquering the BEAST

Understanding the need for more hands-on training, the Air Force recently incorporated Basic Expeditionary Airmen Skills Training (BEAST) to basic training. For most trainees, after Zero Week this is considered the hardest week of training. During this week you will put into practice everything you have learned. You will not be in a classroom environment, but in a simulated, deployed location for the entire week. The main objectives for this training are:

- Familiarize trainees with the pre-deployment process.
- Give trainees leaderships opportunities.
- Prepare trainees for real combat situations.

Another Bus Ride

Your training starts on a bus with all your bags and weapon. Once you arrive at your "deployed" location you will be yelled at and rushed just like when you first arrived at basic training. Once you are off the bus, you will run (carrying all your bags) everywhere you go.

Gear

For this training week you will be issued this gear and equipment:

1. A "flack vest" with armored plates.

2. Knee and elbow pads.

3. Kevlar helmet.

4. Gas mask.

5. Chemical suit.

You will wear your gear at all times, even when using the latrine in the middle of the night. Do not be caught without your gear, and more importantly, do not lose it. The instructors will frequently remind you of the importance of having your gear with you at all times.

The Base

Your new home for the rest of the week will consist of tents. You will be sleeping on a cot with your Flight. Your gear and bags must fit into a foot locker and under your cot. The latrines are located away from the tents. Due to these rugged living conditions, not as much time is spent on cleaning details or having your locker organized.

Training

You will notice that the instructors during this week take a more hands-off approach to training. Your MTI will not be with you for this week. The instructors are there to facilitate the training, while letting you and your Flight have more control. Basically, the instructors will create combat situations and the trainees must work together to pass.

Chemical warfare is a major part of this training. You will be putting your chemical suit on as fast as you can. At anytime, day or night, the alarm can and will sound to prepare for incoming chemical weapons. For this reason, do not go anywhere without your gear.

IED (Improvised Explosive Devices) training takes place while patrolling a road littered with garbage. Recognizing an IED is only half the battle. Once you or another trainee spot an IED, remember to take action and work together. Decide ahead of time who will do what when you find an IED. This will prevent confusion and frustration.

With every Airman expected to take part in base defense, training in defensive fighting has increased in recent years. You will spend many hours in a static defensive fighting position (DFP) waiting to be attacked. Sometimes nothing will happen, and other times you will have three enemy targets coming at you at once. The key to success is to stay alert and to not become complacent. During DFP training you will also learn what types of action to take for different situations, such as when to shoot. The worst thing you can do during this training is to do nothing. Many trainees are unsure of what to do when faced with a particular situation, and in turn take no action at all. Even if you aren't 100% sure of how to respond to a situation, take action and you will have time to discuss it with the instructor after the exercise ends.

You won't get much sleep during this week (plan on no more than two to four hours per night). Just like back in the dorms you will rotate through two-hour shifts watching guard at night. However, the tents are so small that it is hard to sleep through shift changes and other people getting up and putting all their gear on just to go use the latrine.

Four Tips for Conquering the BEAST

Stay motivated. Even though it will seem as if you are waiting and dong nothing, something can happen at any minute.

Work together. This part of training is where you are being tested more than ever to work with the rest of your Flight.

Carry an extra pair of socks. Your feet will sweat a lot and changing your socks during the day will help prevent blisters and infections.

Drink lots of water. You will be outside most of the day wearing a lot of gear, so you will dehydrate much faster than usual.

Chapter 21

Top 15 Most Common "Do Not's" for Trainees

As you might imagine, there are countless things you should not do during basic training. Some are obvious, but it is surprising how many trainees do not use common sense. The following list comprises the top 15 most common problems for recruits in basic training. Memorize this list!

1. Do not talk when you're not supposed to—especially while eating or in formation.

2. Do not shave your head. This goes for prior to arriving at basic training, as well as during basic training.

3. Do not forget your reporting statement.

4. Do not sleep in class.

5. Do not call your M16 a gun. (Call it a weapon or a rifle instead.)

6. Do not say "sorry" or "thank you" to an MTI.

7. Do not scratch, cough, or sneeze while in formation.

8. Do not remove food from the chow hall.

9. Do not lie or sit on your bed unless told otherwise to do so.

10. Do not go anywhere without your mandatory items.

11. Do not carry unauthorized items with you at anytime. (You will know what is not authorized).

12. Do not forget to shave (or not shave on purpose).

13. Do not wear white socks with your ABU uniform.

14. Do not write or mail letters until your MTI gives you permission.

15. Finally, do not do anything that will embarrass your MTI in front of other MTIs.

There are many other things you should not do during basic training. However, these 15 examples are the most common mistakes made by trainees. Don't reinvent the wheel when others have already learned the hard way.

Remember to memorize this list, and your life will be (at least somewhat) easier during basic training.

Chapter 22

Week 7: So Close, Yet so Far

You have just returned from the BEAST, and returning to your dorm feels oddly like coming home. Don't be surprised if your MTI treats you more like you are in your second week of training. For MTIs, when a Flight returns from field training it is similar to when parents have their kids return from summer camp. The kids have picked up bad habits, are more independent, and more likely to disregard some of the house rules.

The first thing you will do directly off the bus is clean your gear. You will have accumulated a week's worth of dirt, mud, and whatever else found its way into your gear. Once everything is clean, including everyone in the Flight, you head in for another week of classroom work. In addition to classroom instruction, your seventh WOT includes a very important event: your final physical fitness evaluation.

Physical Fitness Evaluation

At this point in your training there isn't any more time to increase your push-ups, sit-ups, or run time. Now is when the hours of physical readiness training come into play. Because you were in field training the week prior to this evaluation, you may see a slight decrease in your times and numbers. Hopefully you took it upon yourself to continue doing push-ups and sit-ups on a regular basis during that week.

Sit-ups and Push-ups

During your final evaluation you will be monitored even more closely, so remember these four principles to help you pass.

1. Relax. Clear you mind of everything else.

2. Warm-up properly before starting.

3. Breathe. Remember to exhale when pushing up during push-ups, and sitting up during sit-ups.

4. Focus on form and execution. Make each push-up & sit-up count.

The Run

You will perform the run after the sit-ups and push-ups. The run is self-paced and timed. There will be a large digital clock showing your time as you make your loops around the track. Remember:

Do not return to old habits. People often resort back to how they used to do something when faced with a test or challenge. Use what you learned from Chapter 9 and from your hours of PRT.

Run with a partner. This is a great time to run with someone that you know will challenge your run time. Be sure you do not run with someone that will slow you down.

Push it out. On the last stretch of track on your final loop, sprint to the end. Whether you pass or fail can be determined by seconds.

If you fail any portion of the physical fitness test by a small margin, you will be given a second chance the following day. However, if you fail miserably or fail on your second try, you will be recycled back for the number of weeks deemed necessary for you to get into proper shape.

M9 Qualification

The other major event of Week 7 is shooting/qualifying with the M9 pistol—a recent addition to the new Air Force basic training. The same safety rules that applied to the M16 apply to the M9.

1. Don't touch the weapon until you are told to do so.

2. When handling the weapon, do not point it at anyone—especially an instructor.

3. Do not pull the trigger, except when told to do so.

Be extra cautious when firing the M9. One of the hardest concepts for trainees to grasp during the M9 firing phase is looking from side-to-side with eyes and head only. The tendency when looking to either side is to turn at the waist. This, in turn, results in the trainee pointing the M9 at other trainees or instructors. This, of course, is a safety violation and if you do it you can be kicked off the range.

Qualifying

The same techniques used with the M16 apply:

1. Shoot your own target.

2. Relax by breathing regularly.

3. Shoot on your exhale. Squeeze, don't jerk the trigger.

4. Pretend every shot is a dry fire (no bullet in the weapon). This is particularly true with the M9. The "kick" or recoil is a little more sharp than it is with the M16, and you may tend to compensate by jerking the pistol downward when you pull the trigger.

5. Use your previous shot as a gauge.

Chapter 23

How To . . .

This chapter will teach you some of the basics you need to know before you arrive at basic training. Trainees rarely know any of the six "how to" tips you are about to read. By learning this chapter inside and out before you arrive at basic training, you will have an enormous advantage over most of the other trainees.

How to Stand at Attention

Upon arriving at basic training, one of the very first things you will do is stand at attention. The MTI that greets you will give you a quick lesson on how to properly stand at attention, and if you already know the fundamentals it will save you from receiving "individual attention" right after you step off the bus.

Standing at attention is the position you will use the most during basic training. Practice it in front of a mirror over and over until you have it down perfectly. The following steps show you the correct way to stand at the position of attention. (See photo, page 145.)

Airman at attention

Stand strand straight with your stomach in, chest out and shoulders back.

Head is facing forward and eyes staring directly ahead.

Hands and arms are naturally by the sides of your body.

Cup you hands and have your thumbs touching the first joint of your index finger and alongside the seam of your pants.

Heels are together and toes are pointed out at a 45-degree angle.

Do not be lax. Your body should be ridged, but not tense as to strain you body or restrict breathing or blood flow.

Legs are straight, but knees are not locked.

TIP: Here is a trick to learning the exact position your hands should be in.

Step 1. Take your hand and point it as if it were a gun, (as kids do when playing cops and robbers). Your forefinger is pointing out, your thumb is sticking straight up, and your other fingers are curled in to your palm.

Step 2. As if you are pulling the trigger to the gun, bring your forefinger in all the way joining the other fingers.

Step 3. Lay your thumb flat across your forefinger.

Step 4. Place your hand by your side so your first knuckles are in line with you pants seam. You thumb should be pointing down.

Do not talk, move, sneeze, cough, or even scratch when you are at the position of attention. If rain lands on your face—ignore it. If a mosquito lands on your ear and starts crawling inside—forget about it. If you move from the position of attention, you are showing your MTI that you are undisciplined, and MTIs don't like undisciplined trainees.

In addition to standing at the position of attention in Flight formations, you always stand at the position of attention when addressing your MTI, or when being addressed by an MTI.

How to Stand at Parade Rest

When you are not standing at attention, the other common position is parade rest (see photo, page 139). In Flight formation, this position always follows the position of attention. When "parade rest" is called, execute the following movements from the position of attention.

1. Move your left foot about one foot to the left.

2. Legs should remain straight with your weight evenly distributed.

3. As you move your left foot to the left, place your hands in the center of your lower back just above your belt, palms facing out.

4. Fingers of both hands should be flat and extended out with your thumbs interlocking.

5. Your right hand should be in the palm of your left hand so only the palm of your right hand is visible.

6. Your head and eyes should be straight forward.

7. Remain silent. Changing positions does not mean you can talk.

How and Who to Salute

The act of saluting is a respectful gesture between military personnel. Many civilians (and even some military personnel) do not understand the purpose of the salute. It is important that you do.

The purpose of the salute is to show respect (as when saluting the flag or a military funeral procession), and to show respect for authority (such as when an enlisted Airman salutes an officer). It is tradition and mandatory for the lower ranking individual to salute a higher-ranking individual first.

Airman at parade rest

How to Salute

A salute should be confident, like a handshake. While at the position of attention or walking, raise your right hand until your index finger touches your hat (a.k.a, cover) brim. If you are wearing a flight cap, which has no brim, position your hand about and to the right of

Airman holding a salute

your eye, with your forefinger slightly to the right of your right brow (see photo, above). If you are wearing eyeglasses and a flight cap, use the right tip of your glasses as a benchmark. Hold your upper arm horizontally and you forearm inclined at a 45-degree angle. Slightly turn your hand downward so that neither the back of the hand or the palm is clearly visible. At the same time turn your head toward the person or object (i.e., flag) you are saluting. Hold your salute until the salute is returned, then confidently return you arm to your side.

Warning: You will see many trainees adding their own style to the salute. Do not come up with a style of your own. The salute has strict form and adding a personal "style" shows disrespect. MTIs will notice.

Who to Salute

It is customary to salute all commissioned officers regardless of rank or sex. (See rank structure in Chapter 15). Do not salute non-commissioned officers (i.e., sergeants, except in formation). You will learn more about this in basic training. Commissioned officers also salute each other, with the lower ranking officer saluting first.

Never salute an officer during a field exercise (the BEAST during your 6th week of training) or in combat situations. Doing so is referred to as "sniper check," because it provides the enemy with an idea of who is an officer and who is in charge.

How to Wear a Cover

In the civilian world, a baseball-style cap is worn many different ways. One common way is to wear it with the bill slated upward and folded in an upside down, U shape. In basic training there is only one way to wear your hat or "cover" as you will call it. Your MTI will be looking for

Airman wearing a cover

trainees who fold and bend the bill of their cover. During basic training the bill of your cover should remain straight. Once you graduate basic training, your assigned unit might be more relaxed on how to wear your cover.

To properly wear a military cover, place it on your head straight and level. The bill of the cover should be parallel to the ground, with the base of the bill approximately two inches above the top of the nose.

How to Make Your Bunk

The task of making your bunk to basic training standards is another way to teach the importance of paying attention to detail. Just like with saluting, you need to practice it in order to do it right.

During basic training you are required to have a neatly made bunk at all times. This will not only keep you out of trouble, but it will also show your MTI that you are a "squared away" trainee. Here are a few simple tips for a perfect bunk:

Remember: smooth, neat, and wrinkle free. In order for your bunk to be all of these things, you need to make sure every sheet and blanket, starting with your bottom sheet, is wrinkle-free. The best way to do this is to have another trainee help hold and pull on the opposite end of the sheet.

Every time you tuck your sheet under your bed, make sure it is done tightly. Reach under the bed and pull on the sheets from there.

When laying the blanket down, make sure that it is squared evenly.

You want the same amount of blanket hanging on both sides of your bunk.

Before putting your dust cover on, pull and tighten the blanket one last time.

Want perfect hospital corners? Of course! Follow these tips:

1. Pick up the edge of the sheet/blanket about 12 inches from the foot of the bed.

2. Lift up the sheet/blanket so it makes a diagonal fold.

3. Lay the fold on the mattress.

4. Take the part of the sheet/blanket that is hanging and tuck it underneath the mattress.

5. Lift the fold from the mattress and drop it so it hangs down.

6. Pull it smooth and tuck it under the mattress.

7. Straighten and adjust any bulges or wrinkles.

How to Prepare and Eat a Meal, Ready to Eat (M.R.E)

MRE's are individual meals Airmen eat in the field when no hot chow is available. During your sixth week you will eat them for breakfast and lunch. MRE's come in everything from meatloaf with gravy to Thai chicken to vegetarian meals.

Inside an MRE packet are a series of boxes and small bags. The boxes contain packets of food that can be heated using the heater pouch included in each MRE. Below are step-by-step instructions on how to eat an MRE within the ten minutes you are given for breakfast and lunch during your 6th week of training.

1. Take a mouth full of water from your canteen. Do not swallow it.

2. Tear off the top of the heater pouch. There are two arrows on the pouch; use the top arrow to make your initial tear.

3. Spit your mouthful of water into the heater pouch.

4. Place your packet of food inside the pouch and make sure the packet reaches the bottom of the pouch (so it is flush with the heater).

5. Fold the top of the heater pouch.

6. Put the pouch inside the empty box you took your food packet from.

7. Lean the box on an object, such as a rock or even your foot. While this is heating, eat the rest of your food provided in the MRE.

8. In about five minutes (the recommended time is 10 minutes, but you won't have that long) remove the packet of food from the box, tear the pouch at the notches, and enjoy. (A spoon is optional. It is faster to squeeze the contents into your mouth.)

Chapter 24

Week 8: Congratulations Airman!

Your eighth and final week of basic training (not counting Zero Week) consists of preparing for graduation and taking the final written test. To pass the written test, you must score 70% or higher. To make sure you pass the written test, review the test-taking tips in Chapter 15.

Thursday

Air Force basic training graduation starts on Thursday and ends on Friday of your eighth week.

Airman's Run

The Airman's Run takes place Thursday. You will be running with your Flight and all of the other graduating Flights. This is the first time you will see any of your friends or family if they come for graduation (provided you can spot them in a crowd of people as you run by).

Note: If you have any friends or family coming to graduation, they should go to the Lackland AFB website and search under "basic training." There, they will find information on where to stay, how to get on base, and even a schedule of graduation events.

Directly after the run you will return to your dorm to clean up and change into your dress uniform for the coin ceremony.

The Coin Ceremony

During the Coin Ceremony you will stand with your Flight surrounded by friends and family. Your MTI will present you with the Airman's Coin and shake your hand.

TIP: You will be standing on concrete during the ceremony and your feet will hurt in your new dress shoes. Assuming you have room in your shoes, wear two layers of dress socks to provide extra comfort.

Once the ceremony is over, your friends and family will come down from the bleachers and find you, at which point you are free to go with them.

Honor Graduate Ceremony

If you are an Honor Graduate, you will leave directly from the Coin Ceremony and meet your friends and family at the location of the Honor Graduate Ceremony. This ceremony takes less than hour, and after it ends you are free to go with your friends and family.

Honor Graduate

A small percentage (about 10%) of trainees will graduate from basic training as Honor Graduates. In order to be eligible you must meet the following requirements throughout basic training: (Thunderbolt fitness standards):

	Males	Females
1.5 mile run	9:30 minutes	12:00 minutes
Push-ups	55	32
Sit-ups	60	55
Pull-ups	5	2

Written Tests: You must pass your written tests with a score of 90% or higher on the first try.

Behavior. You cannot have any unfavorable comments or negative counseling on record. (Having a 341 pulled does not necessarily eliminate you from being eligible.)

Friday

The graduation ceremony is on a Friday. You march with your Flight to the parade ground, where you once again stand (this time on grass). Now, finally, your hours and hours of parade (marching) practice come into play. Flight by Flight you will march past the bleachers, past Air Force officials, and past friends and family.

After Graduation

Once graduation is over, you have the weekend to spend with your family on or off base (depending on your MTI's stipulations). MTIs have been known to take away town passes from trainees, requiring them to stay on base the entire weekend. However, if you can, you will want to take this time to get off base and see a little bit of what the outside world looks like around Lackland AFB.

You must return to your dorm by your MTI's specified time. You are still under their authority, and can be recycled.

San Antonio

Downtown San Antonio caters specifically to basic training graduates. Downtown businesses also thrive off newly graduated Airmen, who have been in an extremely controlled environment for the past eight weeks and are ideal candidates for impulse buying.

New Airmen regularly return to the dorm from town pass with new cell phones, laptops, and other electronic devices. However, they forget to take into account that luggage space is restricted.

Spending Tips for the New Airman

- You are better off waiting until you arrive at a tech school location before making any large purchases.

- If a family member wants to buy you something as a graduation gift, see if they can give you the money to buy it later, or mail it to your tech school location.

- If in doubt, do without.

- Pay for events in which you can spend time "with" your family. You will have time to see movies during tech school. Remember, they came to see you.

- The River Walk, which is in the heart of downtown San Antonio, is a destination itself and a great location to spend time with your friends and family. There are numerous restaurants along the River Walk where you can eat as much and as slow as you want.

The Last Night

The last few nights at basic training are notorious for trainees getting wild and crazy. Don't expect to get much sleep. Your last night at basic training will be spent packing and cleaning the dorm. Trainees will be leaving the dorm at different times throughout the night and into the early morning, depending on where they are going for tech school. When it is your time to get on the bus to leave, your MTI will more than likely be there to see you off.

Keep your military bearing at all times. While it is permissible to smile now, don't do anything that will get you held back from tech school. MTIs have had busses turned around to recycle trainees who have shown disrespect toward them at the last minute.

You only go through Air Force basic training once. Make the most of it while you're there by doing everything to the best of your ability.

And remember to have fun.

Chapter 25

Tips for Success

The following list contains numerous tips you should know before beginning basic training. Remember, you can and should log onto www.UltimateBasicTraining.com for more tips, tricks, and tactics for dealing with basic training.

Keep Your Wall Locker Organized at All Times: Whenever you touch something in your wall locker, put it back where it belongs.

Learn Military Time: Learning military time is much easier if you get a watch with an alarm that displays military time.

Initial It: Write your name or initials on absolutely everything you bring to basic training.

Lock It: Always, always, always lock your security drawer, even if you are only walking to the other side of the room.

Tuck Them: Keep your bootlaces tucked inside your boots.

Be Considerate: Make a conscious effort to be considerate of others, especially in times of high stress.

Sleep: As soon as the lights are out, be in bed and sleeping.

Prepare Your E-mail List in Advance: Gather all of your friends and family e-mail addresses and add them to an address book on your e-mail provider. Then, if you get to a computer during one of your base liberties during basic training you can save time by writing one e-mail and sending it to all your friends and family at once.

Phone Cards: Don't leave home without them. Buy plenty of phone cards before you leave for basic training. It is much easier to have one handy when the opportunity to use a phone becomes available, than to beg and borrow from other trainees.

Be the Early Bird: Wake up fifteen minutes earlier than the other trainees (4:15 a.m. instead of 4:30 a.m.). Shave and get dressed. By doing this you will not be quite so rushed, and will reduce some of your stress.

Think "Mature": Try to be the mature trainee in the Flight. The other trainees will respect you more than the others, and will be more willing to help you when you are in need.

Be Quiet! Never speak unless you are asked to talk. If no one has requested you to speak—don't.

Never Lean: Do not lean on a wall or anything else. If you have acquired this habit as a civilian, start breaking yourself of it now.

Hands Out of Your Pockets: Keep your hands out of your pockets. This is another habit you may have to break prior to basic training. Your pockets are there to carry objects, not your hands.

Expect the Unexpected: Do not be upset when you have to wake up in the middle of the night to do exercises. This is a common tactic MTIs use to increase your stress level. Expect the unexpected and you will never be disappointed.

Your Luggage: Take only plain luggage to basic training. Why? MTIs love to pick on trainees who show up with luggage decorated with flowers, designs, or bright colors. Taking plain luggage is another way to keep from standing out.

Carry Your Rifle Everywhere: Whenever your MTI has you carry your rifle, keep it with you at all times. If an MTI finds it unattended (and they will be looking for those trainees who leave them lying around, as many will), you will be "pushing Texas" for a long time.

Expect the Worst: Always expect the worst. If your MTI says you will receive base liberty or a patio break, do not count on it until you actually get it. Often, your liberties and breaks will be taken from you for something someone else did wrong.

Hair Length: For females, your hair must be kept up with no loose ends. Prior to basic training, practice putting your hair up and tight in a short amount of time.

Positive Attitude: Keeping a positive attitude during basic training is your best tool for success.

By studying this list and committing it to memory, you will be well ahead of the game when you arrive at basic training. You will avoid making many of the mistakes made by most other trainees.

Chapter 26

Interview with an MTI

MTIs. Just the name sends shivers down a new recruit's spine (and for good reason, as you will soon find out firsthand). What is an MTI if not a relentless, harsh, persistent machine that will do anything within his power to diminish a trainee's self-esteem and self-respect. Right?

Well . . . No. None of this is really true.

MTIs are thought of this way because they act this way. As a trainee, you must remember MTIs are humans, too. When MTIs are acting relentless and pushing you to try harder, they are simply doing their job—and doing you a favor.

Picture this scenario: You arrive at basic training where MTIs greet you with a smile. They carry your luggage upstairs and introduce you to your maid who will make your bed and fold your clothes. You are then introduced to your Richard Simmons look-a-like "exercise motivator," who will help you shed those unwanted pounds while listening to music of your choice in a comfortable environment. What kind of military would we be if this scenario was anywhere near reality?

Because there are many misconceptions about MTIs, I decided to include this interview to demonstrate that MTIs are indeed human, and that there is a method to their madness. Believe it or not, they are trying to bring out the best in you.

I spoke with Master Sergeant Cecil and asked him a few questions about basic training from an MTI's point of view. He was very clear and concise about what he thinks it takes to succeed in basic training.

After his tour as an MTI, MSSgt Cecil moved into the position of training Air Force recruiters. His experience as an MTI enables him to train recruiters to better prepare new recruits for a successful basic training experience.

The Interview

Q: What personality traits make a trainee successful or unsuccessful?

A: There isn't one personality better than another. If someone wants to succeed they will. If you make up your mind to succeed, then it's only a matter of making it happen by sticking with it.

Q: How can a trainee prepare before coming to basic training?

A: Be as physically fit as possible before coming to basic training. That is the number one problem. Anything else can be fixed or taught. But if you spend the months before basic training playing video games, you won't make it physically. Beyond that, do your research and learn as much as you can, and have an open mind.

Q: From an MTI's viewpoint, how does extending basic training affect you?

A: It gives the trainees more time to apply what we are teaching. Instead of focusing only on little details, the trainees are able to actually have hands-on practice with everything in the lessons.

Q: How can trainees avoid negative attention from an MTI?

A: By doing what you are told, when you are told, and moving with a purpose. Every MTI will tell you that they have had Flights where at the end of training they don't know the name of one trainee. This is because that trainee did what they were supposed to and they didn't have to yell at that trainee all the time. One key way to avoid negative attention is to listen to the message when someone else is receiving negative attention. Then say "Okay, I'll remember to never do that." Also, I always say, listen to the message, not the volume.

Chapter 27

Acronyms and Terms

Each branch of the U.S. Military uses acronyms for almost everything you can imagine, and the Air Force is no different. During basic training, you will learn hundreds of acronym and terms. You will feel as if they expect you to know many of them as soon as you step off the bus. Unfortunately, once you graduate basic training there will be hundreds more you will be expected to learn. Below is a list of acronyms and terms you will hear at basic training. (Marching commands are not included in this list.)

Prepare now! The more you study this list (have a friend or family member test you), the better you will do during basic training. And, you will experience less stress than the guy standing next to you.

Acronyms

AAFES: Army and Air Force Exchange Services
AB: Air Bas
ABU: Airman Battle Uniform
AEF: Air and Space Expeditionary Force
AF: Air Force
AFB: Air Force Base
AFI: Air Force Instruction
AFSC: Air Force Specialty Code

AMC: Air Mobility Command
AMMO: Ammunition
ANG: Air National Guard
ASAP: As Soon As Possible
ASVAB: Armed Forces Vocational Aptitude Test
AWOL: Absent Without Leave
BAH: Base Allowance for Housing
BAS: Base Allowance for Subsistence
BCG: Birth Control Glasses
BMT: Basic Military Training
BX: Base Exchange
CBRNE: Chemical, Biological, Radiological, Nuclear, and High Yield
Explosives.
DOB:Date of Birth
DOD: Department of Defense
DOR: Date of Rank
DOE: Date of Enlistment
EEO: Equal Employment Opportunity
EN: Enlisted
EO: Equal Opportunity
EOD: Explosive Ordnance Disposal
FM: Field Manual
FPCON: Force Protection Condition
FTX: Field Training Exercise
HMMWV: High Mobility Multipurpose -Wheeled Vehicle
IAW: In Accordance With
IED: Improvised Explosive Device.
KP: Kitchen Patrol
LES: Leave and Earnings Statement
LOAC: Law of Armed Conflict
MAJCOM: Major Command
MEPS: Military Entrance Processing Station
MI: Military Intelligence
MRE: Meal Ready to Eat
NBC: Nuclear, Biological, Chemical

NCO: Non-Commissioned Officer

NVG: Night Visions Goggles

OPSEC: Operations Security

OTS: Officer Training School

ORM: Operational Risk Management

POV: Personally Owned Vehicle

POW: Prisoner of War

PRT: Physical Readiness Training

PX: Post Exchange (also BX)

ROE: Rules of Engagement

ROTC: Reserve Officer Training Corps

SGLI: Service Member's Group Life Insurance

SOP: Standard Operating Procedure

SPORTS: Slap, Pull, Observe, Release, Tap, Shoot. (The immediate action taken when your M16 does not fire.)

SSN: Social Security Number

TDY: Temporary Duty

TIG: Time in Grade

TM: Technical Manual

UCMJ: Uniform Code of Military Justice

USO: United Service Organization

UXO: Unexploded Ordnance

VA: Department of Veterans Affairs (formerly Veterans Admin.)

VIP: Very Important Person

WOT: Week of Training

Terms

550 cord: A commonly used rope practical for field use, which has a tensile strength of 550 pounds.

Airbase Defense: Steps taken to ensure the safety of an Air Force Base.

Article 15: A disciplinary statement associated with the loss of rank/pay.

Brass: A shell from a bullet.

Cadence: Songs performed while marching.

Chow Hall: A military cafeteria.

Concertina Wire: Circular barbed wire used to secure boundaries.

Contraband: Unauthorized material.

Convoy: A series of vehicles.

Core Values: The AF's three core values members must live by.

Cover: A hat.

Dependent: Family member of the AF member (spouse or children).

Detail: A miscellaneous duty.

Dream Sheet: A list of bases at which you would prefer to be stationed.

Fraternization: Inappropriate action with the opposite sex.

Front Leaning Rest: Push-ups.

GI Party: A time set aside for a group of people to clean a specific area.

Giant Voice: The base announcement system, used to announce various information including the base security level.

Hazing: Tormenting another trainee by verbal or physical punishment.

High and Tight: A common style of military haircut where the sides are shaved, or nearly shaved, with neatly trimmed hair remaining on the top.

Hospital Corner: A corner of a made-up bed in which the sheets have been neatly and securely folded.

HUA (Hooah): "I hear you," "I understand you," and/or "I acknowledge your statement." (Many meanings have derived from this acronym.)

In Cadence: Counting rhythm called while doing exercises or marching.

Latrine: A bathroom.

Magazine: A metal object used to hold bullets.

Pass: Paperwork associated with allowing military personnel to leave an area for a specific duration of time.

Profile: An order issued by a military doctor that prohibits performing a particular task or function.

Range: A field used to practice firing weapons.

Recycle: To be restarted and sent to a different basic training Flight.

Round: A bullet.

Shakedown: Thorough inspection of an area, or personal belongings.

Smoked: Punishment in the form of physical exercise.

Sound Off: Speak louder.

Square Away: Describes a trainee who has everything in order.

Waiver: A letter allowing a trainee to do or not do something.

Appendix: Workout Logs

Full size downloadable workout logs are available at www.ultimatebasictrainingguidebook.com.

Table 1. Jump Rope Program

Weeks 1 and 2

Time Limit	Style
1 minute	feet together
rest 45 seconds	
1 minute	feet together
rest 45 seconds	
2 minutes	feet together

Weeks 3 and 4

Time Limit	Style
2 minutes	feet together
rest 45 seconds	
2 minutes	alternating legs
rest 45 seconds	
1 minute	left foot only
rest 45 seconds	
1 minute	right foot only

Weeks 5 and 6

Time Limit	Style
2:30 minutes	feet together
rest 1 minute	
2:30 minutes	alternating legs
rest 1 minute	
1:30 minute	left foot only
rest 1 minute	
1:30 minute	right foot only

Weeks 7 and 8

Time Limit	Style
3:00 minutes	feet together
rest 1 minute	
3:00 minutes	feet together
rest 1 minute	
2:00 minutes	feet together
rest 1 minute	
2:00 minutes	feet together

Table 2. Initial Running Assessment

Date: _____

Minimum APFT Score: _____

Time (seconds)

1-mile assessment   = _ _ _ _ _

Estimated 2-mile assessment = _ _ _ _ _ x2= _____

1/4-mile sprint time goal   = _ _ _ _ _ /4= _____ x.80= _____

Table 3. Sprint Day Log (Weeks 1 and 2)

_____ Sprint Time Goal (carried over from Table 2)

Date	Sprint Goal Beat?		Sprint Goal Beat?		Sprint Goal Beat?	
Set 1						
Set 2						
Set 3						
Set 4						
Set 5						
re-done laps						
re-done laps						

Date	Sprint Goal Beat?		Sprint Goal Beat?		Sprint Goal Beat?	
Set 1						
Set 2						
Set 3						
Set 4						
Set 5						
re-done laps						
re-done laps						

Date	Sprint Goal Beat?		Sprint Goal Beat?		Sprint Goal Beat?	
Set 1						
Set 2						
Set 3						
Set 4						
Set 5						
re-done laps						
re-done laps						

Table 4. Evaluation Chart (Weeks 1 and 2)

_____	divided by	_____	X	0.9	___	A
Sum of set 1 from Table 3 (in seconds)		Number of times you completed set 1				
_____	divided by	_____	X	0.9	___	B
Sum of set 2 from Table 3 (in seconds)		Number of times you completed set 2				
_____	divided by	_____	X	0.9	___	C
Sum of set 3 from Table 3 (in seconds)		Number of times you completed set 3				
_____	divided by	_____	X	0.9	___	D
Sum of set 4 from Table 3 (in seconds)		Number of times you completed set 4				
_____	divided by	_____	X	0.9	___	E
Sum of set 5 from Table 3 (in seconds)		Number of times you completed set 5				
A + B + C + D + E / 5		=				New Sprint Time Goal

Table 5. Sprint Day Log (Weeks 3 and 4)

_____ Sprint Time Goal (carried over from Table 4)

Date	Sprint	Goal Beat?	Sprint	Goal Beat?	Sprint	Goal Beat?
Set 1						
Set 2						
Set 3						
Set 4						
Set 5						
Set 6						
re-done laps						
re-done laps						

Date	Sprint	Goal Beat?	Sprint	Goal Beat?	Sprint	Goal Beat?
Set 1						
Set 2						
Set 3						
Set 4						
Set 5						
Set 6						
re-done laps						
re-done laps						

Table 6. Evaluation Chart (Weeks 3 and 4)

_____	divided by	_____	X	0.9	___ A
Sum of set 1 from Table 5 (in seconds)		Number of times you completed set 1			
_____	divided by	_____	X	0.9	___ B
Sum of set 2 from Table 5 (in seconds)		Number of times you completed set 2			
_____	divided by	_____	X	0.9	___ C
Sum of set 3 from Table 5 (in seconds)		Number of times you completed set 3			
_____	divided by	_____	X	0.9	___ D
Sum of set 4 from Table 5 (in seconds)		Number of times you completed set 4			
_____	divided by	_____	X	0.9	___ E
Sum of set 5 from Table 5 (in seconds)		Number of times you completed set 5			
_____	divided by	_____	X	0.9	___ F
Sum of set 6 from Table 5 (in seconds)		Number of times you completed set 6			

A + B + C + D + E + F / 6   =   _____   New Sprint Time Goal

Table 7. Sprint Day Log (Weeks 5 and 6)						
_____ Sprint Time Goal (carried over from Table 6)						
Date	Sprint Goal Beat?		Sprint Goal Beat?		Sprint Goal Beat?	
Set 1						
Set 2						
Set 3						
Set 4						
Set 5						
Set 6						
Set 7						
re-done laps						
re-done laps						
Date	Sprint Goal Beat?		Sprint Goal Beat?		Sprint Goal Beat?	
Set 1						
Set 2						
Set 3						
Set 4						
Set 5						
Set 6						
Set 7						
re-done laps						
re-done laps						

Table 8. Evaluation Chart (Weeks 5 and 6)

	divided by		X	0.9		A
Sum of set 1 from Table 7 (in seconds)		Number of times you completed set 1				

	divided by		X	0.9		B
Sum of set 2 from Table 7 (in seconds)		Number of times you completed set 2				

	divided by		X	0.9		C
Sum of set 3 from Table 7 (in seconds)		Number of times you completed set 3				

	divided by		X	0.9		D
Sum of set 4 from Table 7 (in seconds)		Number of times you completed set 4				

	divided by		X	0.9		E
Sum of set 5 from Table 7 (in seconds)		Number of times you completed set 5				

	divided by		X	0.9		F
Sum of set 6 from Table 7 (in seconds)		Number of times you completed set 6				

	divided by		X	0.9		G
Sum of set 7 from Table 7 (in seconds)		Number of times you completed set 7				

A + B + C + D + E + F + G / 7   =   New Sprint Time Goal

Table 9. Sprint Day Log (Weeks 7 and 8)

_____ Sprint Time Goal (carried over from Table 8)

Date	Sprint	Goal Beat?	Sprint	Goal Beat?	Sprint	Goal Beat?
Set 1						
Set 2						
Set 3						
Set 4						
Set 5						
Set 6						
Set 7						
Set 8						
re-done laps						
re-done laps						

Date	Sprint	Goal Beat?	Sprint	Goal Beat?	Sprint	Goal Beat?
Set 1						
Set 2						
Set 3						
Set 4						
Set 5						
Set 6						
Set 7						
Set 8						
re-done laps						
re-done laps						

Table 10. Evaluation Chart (Weeks 7 and 8)

| _____ | divided by | _____ | X | 0.9 | _____ | A |

Sum of set 1 from Table 9 (in seconds) / Number of times you completed set 1

| _____ | divided by | _____ | X | 0.9 | _____ | B |

Sum of set 2 from Table 9 (in seconds) / Number of times you completed set 2

| _____ | divided by | _____ | X | 0.9 | _____ | C |

Sum of set 3 from Table 9 (in seconds) / Number of times you completed set 3

| _____ | divided by | _____ | X | 0.9 | _____ | D |

Sum of set 4 from Table 9 (in seconds) / Number of times you completed set 4

| _____ | divided by | _____ | X | 0.9 | _____ | E |

Sum of set 5 from Table 9 (in seconds) / Number of times you completed set 5

| _____ | divided by | _____ | X | 0.9 | _____ | F |

Sum of set 6 from Table 9 (in seconds) / Number of times you completed set 6

| _____ | divided by | _____ | X | 0.9 | _____ | G |

Sum of set 7 from Table 9 (in seconds) / Number of times you completed set 7

| _____ | divided by | _____ | X | 0.9 | _____ | H |

Sum of set 8 from Table 9 (in seconds) / Number of times you completed set 8

A + B + C + D + E + F + G + H / 8   =   _____   New Sprint Time Goal

Table 11. Running Program for Long-Run Days	
	Run for a minimum of:
Week 1	20:00 minutes/day
Week 2	22:00 minutes/day
Week 3	24:00 minutes/day
Week 4	26:30 minutes/day
Week 5	28:30 minutes/day
Week 6	31:00 minutes/day
Week 7	33:30 minutes/day
Week 8	36:00 minutes/day

Table 12. *Push-up Evaluation Chart*								
	Number of push-ups required to pass APFT							
Rest	2 minutes between sets							
Weeks 1-3 Duration		Day 1	Day 2	Day 3	Day 4	Day 5	Day 6	Day 7
Set 1	A* 1-minute							
	B* failure							
Set 2	A 1-minute							
	B failure							
Set 3	A 1-minute							
	B failure							
Rest	3 minutes between sets							
Weeks 4-6 Duration		Day 1	Day 2	Day 3	Day 4	Day 5	Day 6	Day 7
Set 1	A 1:30 minutes							
	B failure							
Set 2	A 1:30 minutes							
	B failure							
Set 3	A 1:30 minutes							
	B failure							
Rest	4 minutes between sets							
Weeks 7-8 Duration		Day 1	Day 2	Day 3	Day 4	Day 5	Day 6	Day 7
Set 1	A 2-minutes							
	B failure							
Set 2	A 2-minutes							
	B failure							
Set 3	A 2-minutes							
	B failure							

A*regular push-ups

B*kneeling diamond push-ups

Table 13. *Sit-up Evaluation Chart*								
	_____Number of sit-ups required to pass APFT							
Rest 2 minutes between sets								
Weeks 1-3 Duration	Day 1	Day 2	Day 3	Day 4	Day 5	Day 6	Day 7
Set 1 A* 1-minute								
B* failure								
Set 2 A 1-minute								
C* failure								
Rest 3 minutes between sets								
Weeks 4-6 Duration	Day 1	Day 2	Day 3	Day 4	Day 5	Day 6	Day 7
Set 1 A 1:30 minutes								
B failure								
Set 2 A 1:30 minutes								
C failure								
Rest 4 minutes between sets								
Weeks 7-8 Duration	Day 1	Day 2	Day 3	Day 4	Day 5	Day 6	Day 7
Set 1 A 2-minutes								
B failure								
Set 2 A 2-minutes								
C failure								
A*regular sit-ups								
B*abdominal crunches								
C*upper-half crunches								

Table 14. 8-Week Fitness Chart								
	Week 1	Week 2	Week 3	Week 4	Week 5	Week 6	Week 7	Week 8
Day 1	A	B	C (24 m)	B	D	B	C (33:30 m)	B
Day 2	B	D	B	C (26:30 m)	B	D	B	C (36 m)
Day 3	C (20 m)	B	D	B	C (28:30 m)	B	D	B
Day 4	B	C (22 m)	B	D	B	C (31 m)	B	D
Day 5	D	B	C (24 m)	B	D	B	C (33:30 m)	B
Day 6	B	D	B	C (26:30 m)	B	D	B	C (36 m)
Day 7	C (20 m)	B	D	B	C (28:30 m)	B (31 m)	D	B

A = 1-mile Assessment

B = push-ups and sit-ups

C = Long-run Day

D = Sprint Day

M = Minutes

Index

About the Author

Nicholas Van Wormer graduated as an honor student in 2007 from Air Force basic military training. Since that time, Senior Airman Van Wormer has served in multiple missions in support of Operation Iraqi Freedom. These missions included deploying to Baghdad, Iraq, in 2009-2010 and stateside base law enforcement. Nick serves in the Air Force National Guard (Security Forces/Police unit) and works for Wegmans in the Asset Protection Department. Nick was born and grew up in Spokane, Washington, and graduated from Belhaven University with a degree in theater. He lives in Brockport, New York with his wife Vanessa.